ROYAL
CHILDHOODS

By the same author
Charles I: The Personal Monarch

ROYAL
CHILDHOODS

CHARLES CARLTON

ROUTLEDGE & KEGAN PAUL
LONDON, BOSTON AND HENLEY

First published in 1986
by Routledge & Kegan Paul plc

14 Leicester Square, London, WC2H 7PH, England

9 Park Street, Boston, Mass. 02108, USA, and

Broadway House, Newtown Road,
Henley on Thames, Oxon RG9 1EN, England

Set in Garamond, 11 on 13pt
by Input Typesetting London,
and printed in Great Britain
by Thetford Press, Thetford, Norfolk

Library of Congress Cataloging in Publication Data

Carlton, Charles, 1941–

Royal childhoods.
Bibliography: p.
Includes index.
1. Great Britain—Kings and rulers—Biography.
2. Great Britain—Kings and rulers—Children—Biography.
I. Title.
DA281.C37   1986   941'.009'92 [B]   85-8268

British Library CIP data available

ISBN 0-7102-0185-0

For
ABIGAIL AND VICTORIA

CONTENTS

PLATES

ACKNOWLEDGMENTS

I would like to thank Andrew Best, Michael Bloch, Murray Downs, Peter Kaufman and Clay Griffith for reading and commenting on various chapters, and Peter Fry and Andrew Wheatcroft for their most welcome encouragement. My debt to my wife Caroline for criticizing and revising the various drafts with her usual thoroughness and tenacity is as great as ever. I owe a special vote of thanks to Annette Thomlinson and Terri Anderson for typing nigh illegible scripts. I am most grateful to Terry Quigley for obtaining the illustrations, acknowledgment for which is as follows: Plates 16, 20, 25, 30, 35, 36, 37, 40, 41, 42, 43, 44, 45, 47, 48, 50 and 52 are reproduced by gracious permission of Her Majesty the Queen. I should like to thank the following for permission to reproduce the other plates: Lady Ashcombe for Plate 1 (on view at Sudeley Castle, Winchcombe, Glos); BBC Hulton Picture Library for Plates 64 and 65; The British Library for Plates 5, 7, 8, 9 and 13; The British Museum for Plate 10; the British Tourist Authority for Plate 11; Camera Press London for Plates 67 and 69; Central Press Photos Ltd for Plate 68; City of Bristol Museum and Art Gallery for Plate 29; John Freeman Ltd for Plate 50; Giraudon, Paris, for Plate 2; Michael Holford for Plates 4 and 6; The Illustrated London News Picture Library for Plate 62; Kunsthistorisches Museum, Vienna, for Plate 19; The Metropolitan Museum of Art, New York, for Plate 12 (The Cloisters Collection, Purchase 1934. [34.115.4ab]): The Museum of Fine Arts, Basel (Department of Prints and Drawings) for Plate 21; The National Portrait Gallery, London, for Plates 17, 18, 22, 23, 24, 26, 28, 31, 32, 34, 38, 39, 46, 63; Popperfoto for Plates 51, 53, 54, 55, 56, 57, 58, 59, 60, 61 and 66; Mrs P. A. Tritton, Parham Park, Pulborough, Sussex, for Plate 33; The Victoria and Albert Museum for Plates 3 and 49; The Wallace Collection for Plate 27; The Dean and Chapter of Westminster for Plate 15; The Dean and Chapter of Worcester Cathedral for Plate 14.

I

THE MORNING OF ROYALTY

The childhood shows the man,
As Morning shows the day.
> John Milton, *Paradise Regained*,
> Book 4, lines 219–20

Ever since the beginnings of human society people have realized the critical importance of childhood and adolescence in shaping adult life. Individuals have invested time, effort and money on bringing up their children not merely to satisfy their own parental urges, but from the intellectual recognition that a successful childhood will enhance their offspring's careers. Collectively societies have emphasized child-rearing because they know they need to produce sufficient capable people to ensure the group's survival.

In recent years psychologists have confirmed what the poets have told us, and what every parent instinctively knows. Stimulated by the work of Sigmund Freud they have shown the crucial importance of a child's earliest years, of its relations to father, mother, siblings, and peers. Worried parents have responded by sending children in droves to kindergartens and play groups, and by buying so many child manuals that the works of Dr Spock and his ilk have consistently made it to the bestseller lists.

Childhood, of course, is not the only vitally important stage in forming an adult personality. Just as a child has to learn to be, to find out how to exist in this world by developing basic skills such as speech and the avoidance of obvious dangers like fire, so an adolescent has to answer the question 'What will I become?' Perhaps this process is more painful for adolescents, for it takes place at a time when they are fully aware of the strains of sexual and emotional maturity. Clearly the first is a chemical, and a physical change, while the latter (which has been described as an 'identity crisis'), combines deep-rooted feelings towards parents with the intellectual challenge of learning new skills in order to make one's mark in the world.

Childhood and adolescence are two distinct phases leading to adulthood. In the first, individuals have to learn to look after themselves, albeit at a rudimentary level. During the second they become capable of reproduction, and thus have to be ready to look after others. While both stages have a common purpose – that of growing up – they lack a common appellation. This means that we are often forced to use childhood in an extended sense to describe the far longer period of coming to age.

The childhood of kings and queens has always been recognized as especially significant. Contemporaries frequently recorded the details of royal childhoods, while ignoring those of common folk. The education of princes and princesses has often been a matter for public debate, and an opportunity for the professional advancement of their tutors. In much the same way dynastic hopes, even the fear of civil war, have hung on the health of a young heir, prompting doctors to chronicle it in exhaustive detail.

The youths of heirs and heiresses have been recorded because they were destined for greatness. Perhaps therein lies the fascination of monarchy. Most sovereigns are not inherently great men or women. Unlike a modern prime minister, or president, they do not have to struggle for years, beating rivals, cajoling voters, and making alliances in order to achieve power. They are, instead, men and women, as ordinary as most of us, cast into a world of fame and fortune by an accident of birth as fantastic as that well-nigh universal dream of being rescued from our mundane world by marrying some fairy prince or princess.

Yet only fifteen of the forty monarchs who have ruled England since 1066 were born in the direct and certain line of succession. All princesses could never be sure that their parents would not produce a son to displace them. Younger sons had to wait for the death of an elder brother. Eleven of the twenty-nine monarchs to rule England between 1066 and 1688 gained the throne by force of arms. In some cases an unhappy childhood pushed them into seizing power to compensate for early deprivation: William I, who conquered England in 1066, was illegitimate. Conversely a mother's intense love could give a son enough self-confidence to induce real success, while a father's indifference, even scorn, could make an heir strive desperately for power to redeem himself.

That eight of the eleven kings who seized the English throne had unhappy childhoods does not, of course, mean that their earliest years determined the rest of their lives. Bright mornings can often precede stormy evenings: little in life is inevitable. On the other hand childhood can explain adult behaviour. People learn from the past, responding to a situation by drawing on the experience of previous, similar situations, often modifying their responses but rarely changing them radically. Even a new experience, such as a good marriage, or a wise counsellor, may only appear to make a dramatic change, for an individual's decision to marry well or take good advice is usually made with earlier lessons in mind.

Nature then is as important as nurture. Indeed, recent research on identical twins separated at birth suggests that the former may be the more significant. Drastic character differences between brothers such as Richard I and John, Prince Arthur and Henry VIII, Prince Henry and Charles I, Prince Eddy and George V, Edward VIII and George VI, clearly demonstrate the significance of genes. Yet genetic explanations of an individual's behaviour, like those rooted in generalizations about national character or breeding, tend to be too broad to have much meaning. As any parent will tell you, gene pools are so diverse that they seem to produce an infinite variety of characteristics in children.

The lives of the eight sovereigns chosen for further study in this book will readily demonstrate this point. These six men and two women were not selected because their childhoods were typical – it is doubtful if there is such a thing as a typical royal childhood. They have been chosen because their reigns were interesting and crucial in the development of the British monarchy. Some, such as Elizabeth I and Victoria, were resounding successes; others, such as John or Edward VIII, crashing failures. Some, like William the Conqueror, had troubled childhoods; others, like George III, happy ones. The list includes intelligent people such as Elizabeth I, headstrong ones such as Charles I, figures as complacent as George III, and as self-willed as Edward VIII. Taken together all eight of them show how both the monarchy and childhood have changed over the last nine centuries.

It was not until the Renaissance that childhood emerged as a separate, precious stage in human development. The earliest surviving childhood portrait of a prince dates from about 1495 and shows Henry, Duke of York, aged four or five. Later, as Henry VIII, this rather placid-looking boy used paintings to stress the dynastic virtues of the Tudors, both to ensure a legitimate succession and to match the growing family aspirations of the gentry (Plate 1). This theme reappeared four centuries later when another new and insecure middle class, produced by the Industrial Revolution, sought in the royal family confirmation of their own virtues of domestic respectability. Recently, in a changing world that has seen the rapid loss of a massive and proud empire, subjects still look to the royal family as the rock that epitomizes standards – a Gibraltar made perhaps even more precious since those standards have not been met in their own families' lives.

For this reason changes in the royal family have tended to lag behind those of society, even the aristocracy. Victoria's subjects were far more flexible in their morality (so long as they kept it discreet) than was their sovereign. In much the same way divorce became tolerated in the more distant reaches of the royal family, like that of the Earl of Harewood in 1967, long after it was accepted in the rest of the land. Public expectations of the royal family have never been consistent. While it has served as the guardian of moral standards long since gone, it has also been the beneficiary of immoral pleasures way beyond the hopes (although not the fantasies) of most of its subjects. Today as in earlier times loyal subjects vicariously enjoy the pleasures of princes.

Just as royal families and morality have been atypical, so have royal childhoods. Kings and queens played little part in the daily upbringing of their offspring. Like all aristocrats they left that task to wet-nurses, nannies and tutors. Until Prince Charles went to Hill House School in 1957, heirs to the throne had been brought up without the company and cruelty of school companions. Perhaps the greatest difference between royal childhoods and those of all other children, no matter how nobly born, has been a profound sense of ambivalence. Those appointed to bring them up and educate in them the craft of kingship, have always realized that the bottom they birch today will tomorrow sit upon the throne. Thus no young prince or princess could fail to sense that the adults they had to please and obey also desperately wanted to please them.

This ambivalence became even more poignant as heirs had to come to terms with their parents. For princes the Oedipal tensions that all sons feel towards their fathers is heightened by the fact that like the Oedipus of Greek legend they too must wait for their fathers to die before they can inherit and fulfil their ordained adult role. Wanting and yet fearing a father's death produces intense guilt. In addition eldest sons might wonder if their younger brothers secretly wish them dead so they can inherit, while younger sons could at the same time fear the elders' demise, and yet resent the accident of birth that

1 *Allegorical painting of Henry VIII and his children*, artist unknown. One of the earliest paintings of the royal family, this piece of Elizabethan propaganda underscores both the legitimacy of the Tudor dynasty and simple family virtues. Mary Tudor is shown holding Philip of Spain's hand, as Mars stands behind them ready to strike. On the other side Elizabeth embraces Peace whilst being attended by Plenty

condemns them to a life of meaningless obscurity on the fringes of power, bereft of much chance of a worthwhile career. Those such as Edward VII or George III's royal dukes, condemned to wait for decades for the chance of power, often revert to a life of endless adolescence, relieved only by an almost neurotic pursuit of women, food, money, and empty self-gratification.

Since the Conquest the role of the monarchy as a political institution has altered far more than that of the family. No longer could a fatal arrow in a king's eye change a nation's whole way of life. Now an assassin's bullet would produce national mourning, relieved by a reassuring sense of continuity. While the family may be decreased in size, ceasing to be an extended institution, its importance in child-rearing has increased, even as the role of others such as teachers, doctors and lecturers has grown. At the same time, the power of the monarch has faded from being the omnipotent, divinely ordained ruler, to that of a figurehead who can do no wrong because he or she can do nothing significant in his or her own right. Thus the qualities demanded from a monarch have changed drastically over the centuries. Had a time machine allowed Charles I to become a twentieth-century king, he might well have died in his bed, a much-lamented President of the Royal Academy. Had the first Elizabeth been able to change places with the second the results for sixteenth- and twentieth-century England could have been disastrous. Although such speculation is as intriguing as it is unproductive, it still underscores an important fact – that the qualities demanded from a royal childhood today are very different from those valued throughout most of the history of the British crown.

Modern monarchs need passivity rather than drive, ordinariness instead of brilliance, patience as opposed to ambition. While they should not be stupid, they can't be too bright. They should not be lazy, and yet, faced with a lifetime of red boxes containing state papers to read, comment on, and not act upon, they should not be too energetic.

Because monarchs have become in many ways anachronisms this balance between mediocrity and excellence has grown all the more necessary. When the king was head of the feudal pyramid or ruled by divine right, subjects could more readily accept a poor sovereign, for the office and not the office-holder was the apex of the real political world. Today, sovereigns chosen on the archaic basis of primogeniture have become a contradiction in a democracy founded on principles of equality and opportunity. Anachronisms can be attractive. Monarchy works because logically it should not work – its appeal is to magic, to the heart and not the head. And the moment that the modern royal family forgets that fact it will immediately be driven from the pomp and circumstance of centuries of office to a life of foreign exile as meaningless as the Duke of Windsor's. What the chances are of that happening no one can foretell: yet one thing is sure – that they lie in good part within the experiences of past royal childhoods and the hopes of those to come.

II

WILLIAM I

According to a twelfth-century chronicler, Robert, Duke of Normandy, fell in love at first sight with Herleve (sometimes known as Arlette), when he spied the maid washing clothes in the stream that flowed beside her father's tannery at the foot of Falaise Castle. He took her back to his chamber, and that night, having conceived their first child, she dreamed that a tree sprang from her womb, its branches growing and growing until they covered not just Normandy, but all England as well. There is, of course, no historical truth in this story – at least not in the literal sense. For one thing, Herleve's father was far too prosperous a businessmen to let his daughter do the family's wash; but at another level the legend does contain a significant figurative truth, made all the more important by the lack of first-hand evidence. No personal letters from William have survived, neither have any transcripts of his speeches taken down by contemporaries. Their view of the past was very different from ours. It was not to be found in archives carefully constructed for the edification of posterity, but in stories, legends, or formal speeches (particularly ones given from a death bed), which they believed captured the essential rather than the literal truth. That various sources, among them Norman chroniclers and the weavers of the Bayeux Tapestry (the official military history of the Norman Invasion), agreed, confirms not what actually happened, but what the Normans, and William in particular, thought took place. And for a biographic study the subject's perception of events is as important – if not more significant – than historical reality itself.

Of one historic fact there can be no doubt. William was born a bastard, his parents' union being neither sanctioned by the church nor blessed by society. The chances of the child Herleve supposedly conceived that night in Falaise Castle ruling Normandy, let alone England, were infinitely remote. At the same time, William's illegitimacy may well have provided the impetus both for his struggle to

7

2 *Falaise Castle.* Here William was born in 1027 or 1028, the bastard son of Robert, Duke of Normandy, and Herleve, reputedly a tanner's daughter. William probably spent his earliest years in Falaise. After his father died in 1035 baronial revolts forced William to flee for his life

3 *Bayeux Tapestry*. During his youth William had to fight long and hard to regain his patrimony, and then secure Normandy from external attacks. The Bayeux tapestry shows him attacking Dol Castle in Brittany, as Duke Conan II escapes by sliding down a rope

4 *Bayeux Tapestry*. William is shown administering an oath of allegiance to Harold, Earl of Wessex, who takes it with one hand on the Bible and the other on a chest of relics. William used this story to justify his conquest of England

5 *Edward the Confessor.* King of England from 1043 to 1066, Edward was an extraordinarily saintly man who refused to consummate his marriage to Harold's sister, Edith. While this story enhanced his reputation with contemporaries, and helped him become a saint, it left England with a succession problem. When he died childless in January 1066, Harold Hardraada, King of the Danes, tried – but failed – to conquer England. William managed to do so at the battle of Hastings

gain Normandy after his father died when he was about eight, and for his determination to embark on the desperate adventure of invading England.

Another chronicler tells a legend that supports the connection between William the Bastard (as he was called by contemporaries) and William the Conqueror (as he is known in English history). When he was about eighteen he asked Count Baldwin V of Flanders if he might marry his daughter Matilda. This high-born young woman, the granddaughter of the King of France, scornfully replied that she would wed no bastard. William, who was a huge man, six foot tall, immediately rode to Bruges, entered the palace and forced his way into Matilda's room, where he beat and kicked the 4 foot 2 inch girl. After he left she took to her bed, vowing to marry no one but her conqueror.

Apart from his illegitimacy little else is known about William's earliest years. Even the date of his birth is a matter of dispute. He may have been born as early as 1027, although recent scholarship inclines towards the autumn of 1028. His mother probably continued to live with Robert for a couple more years, having another child, Adelaide, by him. Herleve may even have nursed William herself, or had her family bring him up at Falaise. Certainly they profited from the liaison. Her father, Fulbert, was made the duke's steward. Her brothers Osbert and Walter became substantial enough to serve as witnesses for several important charters. When William was about two or three – a critically important age in any child's development – Robert married Herleve off to Herluin, Vicomte of Conteville, a prominent vassal, by whom she promptly had a son, Odo.

As the product of a youthful dalliance William's position in his mother's new family was uncertain, even if Herluin benefited from the relationship as had Fulbert. William had few expectations until late 1034, when Robert announced that he was going on a pilgrimage to Jerusalem, and called a meeting of his magnates to browbeat them into accepting his bastard as his heir. 'He is little,' declared the duke, 'but will grow if God so wills, and grow better.'[1] Many barons objected to the idea of a pilgrimage. Having fought to help Robert seize Normandy following the sudden death of his elder brother, Duke Richard III, in August 1027, they had no wish to see Normandy return to anarchy. They only accepted William's nomination after being persuded by Archbishop Robert of Rouen. All recognized that going on a pilgrimage was one of the strongest impulses of the day – particularly, whispered the malicious, on the part of a duke who had poisoned his elder brother. Agreeing on a temporary heir, just in case Robert died before he could return home to marry and raise legitimate sons, was a perfectly sensible precaution.

It turned out to be a valid one. In July 1035 Robert died at Nicea in Asia Minor on his way back from Jerusalem. With Archbishop Robert's help the barons accepted William as Duke of Normandy. So did Henry I, King of France, to whom William may well have personally sworn homage as a vassal. Equally important, Duke Richard III's son, Nicholas, did not contest the succession, preferring to remain in the various monasteries to which Robert had committed him on seizing power.

The death of Archbishop Robert of Rouen on 16 March 1037 removed the one man in Normandy capable of keeping the barons in check during William's minority. Conditions deteriorated precipetously. Rebellions became commonplace. Rape, looting, and pillaging infested Normandy, as if the Vikings had returned to ply their old barbarous ways. Many of William's supporters perished in the anarchy. Count Allen III of Brittany died suddenly in mysterious circumstances. Ralph de Gacé, one of Archbishop Robert's sons, had Gilbert, Duke Robert's friend and William's tutor, assassinated. Turold, a former tutor, was murdered. Osbern, William's steward, died in an affray fought in the duke's own chamber. The boy's uncle Walter (Herleve's brother) often had to spend the night on guard in William's room, and on several occasions baronial plots forced them to seek refuge in peasant hovels. Only luck, and the realization that his death might invite French or Angevin intervention, helped William survive what a biographer called 'a terrible childhood' lived during 'one of the darkest periods of Norman history'.[2]

The nadir was reached in 1046, when William came of age. Seeking to keep central power weak, a baronial faction led by Guy of Burgundy, attempted to seize William at Valognes. Forewarned, the young man escaped. Riding in desperate haste he managed to ford the Vire estuary at low tide, outrunning his pursuers to reach the safety of Falaise. He appealed to Henry I, whom he found at Poissy, throwing himself at the king's feet to claim the protection that was due all faithful vassals. Worried by growing anarchy in Normandy, and grateful for the help Duke Robert had given him and his mother in 1031 when a similar baronial coup had forced them from their lands, Henry invaded Normandy in early 1047. Marching rapidly via Caen he routed William's enemies at Val-ès-Dunes, driving the survivors to watery graves in the nearby river Orne.

Although William fought bravely at Val-ès-Dunes, his rule was far from secure, for the victory was, in fact, won by French rather than Norman knights. So William had to pardon all but one of the rebels, and call an ecclesiastical council at Caen to proclaim a Truce of God, prohibiting private wars between Wednesday evening and Monday morning, and during Advent, Lent, Easter, and Pentecost. Even though the truce helped restore order in Normandy, William had to spend three years starving Guy of Burgundy out of his castle at Brionne. He consolidated his hold over Normandy by building castles throughout the dukedom, cultivating the church and the barons, and forging a marriage alliance with Flanders.

William's successes aroused the enmity of neighbours. Geoffrey Martel, Count of Anjou, tried to expand into Southern Normandy, and after William checked his advance by capturing Alençon and Domfront castles, allied with Henry I in 1052 for a joint invasion.

Two years later William eventually defeated the French at the battle of Mortemer, a victory as significant as that of Val-ès-Dunes. The deaths of Geoffrey Martel and Henry I in 1060 confirmed William's hegemony, particularly as the eight-year-old king of France, Philip I, became the ward of Count Baldwin, William's father-in-law.

For the next half-dozen years William consolidated his position by continuing to strengthen links with baronial families, cooperating with Bishop Lanfranc to build up the church, and invading Brittany to protect his western frontier. At times it seemed as if he were preparing to inherit an almost forgotten legacy promised him many years before.

The events of 1051 are complex, and open to several interpretations, particularly as all the contenders for the English crown claimed that Edward the Confessor had promised them (or their father) the throne. Still the fact remains that William was convinced, and Norman chroniclers all agreed, that in the late spring of 1051 Edward named William as his successor to the throne of England. Robert of Jumièges may well have brought the proposal to Normandy on his way to Rome, where he received the pallium (his symbol of office) as Archbishop of Canterbury on 21 June. There is, however, no evidence to support the assertion of the *Anglo-Saxon Chronicle* that William personally came to England to accept the donation. Edward's promise seems to have goaded Godwin, Earl of Wessex, into refusing to appear before the king's court to answer charges arising from an affray at Dover. Instead the earl went into exile on the Continent, where he raised an army; he then invaded England, and purged Edward's councils of all Norman advisers except for the Bishop of London, and one Ralph the Timid. For the next fourteen years Godwin, and then his son Harold of Wessex, dominated English affairs.

Edward still retained sufficient influence to send Harold to France in 1064; in order – so William believed – to confirm the 1051 promise. After setting sail from Bosham in Sussex, Harold was blown ashore by adverse winds near the mouth of the river Somme, where the local magnate, Count Guy of Ponthieu, arrested him. William intervened to have Harold freed from Guy's dungeons, and personally escorted the earl as an honoured guest into Rouen. Soon afterwards, in a ceremony the Bayeux Tapestry dramatically recorded, Harold swore with one hand on a Bible, and the other over a chest of relics, to represent William at Edward's court, to maintain garrisons of Norman knights in England, and do all he could to ensure William's succession. Later stories that Harold was forced to make this promise in return for his freedom, or was tricked into doing so, seem doubtful. Relations between Harold and William appeared cordial as they campaigned together that summer against Count Conan II of Brittany. Harold's decisive actions following Edward's death on 5 January 1066 were certainly not those of a simpleton capable of being duped by a Bible and a box of saints' bones. The next day, 6 January, the Witan elected Harold King of England, and Archbishop Ealdred of York crowned him in Westminster Abbey, the church that Edward had founded, and in which he was buried that same day. Then Harold mobilized the fleet and militia to fight to keep the crown he had seized so decisively.

The first attempt to take it away from him came on 18 September, when a huge armada of over three hundred ships, commanded by Harold Hardraada, King of Norway, and Tosti, Harold of Wessex's estranged brother, sailed up the Humber and landed at Riccall, ten miles south of York, which they captured two days later. Straight away Harold force-marched his troops up the Great North Road, surprising the Norseman at Stamford Bridge, astride the river Derwent, seven miles east of York. Here on 25 September he won a spectacular victory. Harold Hardraada and Tosti were slain: it needed but twenty-four ships to take the survivors back home.

King Harold had little time to savour his triumph, for very soon afterwards he heard that William had landed at Pevensey in Sussex

on 28 September. So he regrouped and marched his troops south
again, stopping briefly in London before confronting the Norman
invaders just outside Hastings on 14 October.

William's reaction to Harold's seizure of the English throne was
equally decisive. According to a Norman chronicler, on hearing of
the coup 'the duke at once sent messengers to Harold urging him to
desist from this mad policy'.[3] Another chronicler surely reflected
William's feelings when he described Harold as 'stained with vice, a
cruel murderer, purse proud, and puffed up with the profits of
pillage, an enemy of justice and all good'.[4]

Persuading the Norman magnates to punish such malignancy was
far from easy, and according to a later tradition it was only the
eloquence of William fitz Osbern which convinced them that an
invasion was feasible. The barons accepted Matilda as regent during
William's absence, and his fourteen-year-old son, Robert, as heir
just in case the duke, like his father, died whilst on a foreign adventure. During the spring and summer of 1066 William and his barons
assembled an army of ten to twelve thousand men, and built some
four hundred ships. Since these vessels were in fact little better than
flat-bottomed landing barges made from unseasoned timber, and
capable of sailing only with the wind, the expedition had to wait in
St Valéry harbour for favourable weather. Eventually it came on 27
September, the usual westerlies shifting south, permitting the fleet
to set sail that evening. William led the invasion force aboard the
inappropriately named *Mora* (the Latin for 'delay'), for at dawn he
found that his boat had outrun the rest of the fleet and was alone in
the middle of the English Channel. Calmly the duke ordered a great
feast to be prepared, with several bumpers of spiced wine, and 'dined
in good spirits as if he was in a room of his own house'.[5] He kept
up his men's morale until the other ships were sighted coming over
the horizon. That day they landed at Pevensey Bay (which has since
silted up), and captured the port of Hastings on 28 September. On
hearing that Harold was rapidly approaching, William moved his
men out of the town to meet him on a ridge astride the London
road seven miles to the north.

At about 9:30 on the morning of Saturday 14 October, battle
commenced. Both sides, it seems, were equally matched, with
roughly seven thousand men apiece, having similar armour and
weapons. The pride of Harold's army was the housecarls, an elite
troop of mounted infantry, perhaps the best soldiers in Europe, and
he had the advantage of a far better position on top of a hill, which

his men, who fought on foot, augmented by linking their kite-shaped shields to form a protective wall. William for his part had cavalry and superior archers, and his men were far fresher and more determined than Harold's troops, exhausted by their forced march from the North. 'You fight not merely for victory but also for survival,' the duke warned his troops; 'there is no road for retreat.'[6] Then he ordered the Breton infantry on the left to attack under covering fire from his archers. The Anglo-Saxons rapidly pushed them back down the ridge, as the arrows glanced off their shields. With equal ease they repulsed a Norman cavalry charge in the centre. Throughout the day William's position deteriorated. At one stage his men started to retreat in panic when they heard the rumour that he had been killed, and he was only able to rally them by removing his helmet and shouting to his men (as well as the enemy's archers), 'Look at me well. I am still alive, and by the grace of God shall yet prove victor.'[7] Towards evening, in a last desperate throw, the Normans may have repeated the ruse they had used effectively in Sicily six years before, feigning a retreat to trick the enemy into breaking ranks. Anyway, as the Anglo-Saxons charged down the hill, the Norman cavalry countered. Learning that Harold and his brothers had been killed, the Anglo-Saxons lost heart, and the Normans slew them in their thousands. William of Poitiers, the Norman Chronicler, quite rightly boasted that 'William in a single day so crushed the English that afterwards they never dared again face him in battle.'[8]

The conquest was far from complete. Moving slowly and inexorably, William marched in a broad sweep around London, which he entered two months later, to be crowned King of England on Christmas Day 1066. Sporadic resistance continued for nearly six years, with the guerilla campaign of Hereward the Wake in the Fens, and the far more serious opposition in the North which was savagely quelled in 1069–70.

Without doubt the Norman Conquest was the most significant event in English history in the millennium between the conversion to Christianity and the reformation. Although historians have debated its effects (sometimes with a ferocity almost akin to that displayed at Hastings), all agree that the Conquest destroyed the old Anglo-Saxon nobility, replacing them with a new alien Norman elite; England became linked with Latin and not Scandinavian Europe; French became the dominant language; within a generation there was hardly an Anglo-Saxon church or bishop left in the land,

6 *The White Tower, the Tower of London,* from a late fifteenth-century manuscript in the British Museum. The Normans built castles all over England to consolidate their conquest. William and his four or five thousand followers expelled or killed the old Anglo-Saxon nobility, divided their lands, and imposed on the English people a new form of feudalism, culture, laws, and administration, while greatly strengthening links with the Continent. The White Tower, begun in 1078, is a splendid example of the great stone keeps which symbolized the new order

7 The king in council. William augmented the royal administration. Using an elaborate system of courts he and his successors made the king the ultimate source of justice, and – as the

18

hanging on the right of this illuminated manuscript shows – of punishment. Few events have
had such a profound effect on the history of England as the conquest of William the Bastard

and William greatly strengthened the power of the crown. 'He laid taxes on the people very severely,' lamented the *Anglo-Saxon Chronicle*, 'and built castles far and wide throughout this country, and distressed the wretched folk, and always after that it grew much worse.'[9]

But if the Norman Conquest was a disaster for the Anglo-Saxons, for William it was a personal triumph, the roots of which may to a large extent be found in his early life.

Merely to survive his childhood and adolescence, and retain his patrimony, William had to have personal qualities and a determination of the highest order. In its turn overcoming such difficulties honed William's drive and skills, fitting him for the conquest of England. For instance, at the battle of Hastings, where he had three horses killed under him, he displayed the same courage that turned the French victory at Val-ès-Dunes into a personal triumph. William had been hardened in the crucible of youth. 'Thus from my childhood, I have been continually involved in numberless troubles,' he confessed in the deathbed speech the chronicler Ordericus Vitalis attributed to him.[10] 'The Normans,' he thought, 'when under the rule of a kind but firm master are a most valiant people. But in other circumstances they bring ruin on themselves by rending each other. They are eager for rebellion, ripe for tumults, and ready for any sort of crime. . . . I have learnt this by much experience.' Experience had also taught him the advantages of guile, intrigue, trickery and deceit, and never to trust anyone fully. 'My nearest friends, my own kindred, who ought to have defended me at all hazards against the whole world formed conspiracies against me, and nearly stripped me of the inheritance of my fathers,' he said. Not surprisingly William learnt to survive through the use of terror. The barbarous treatment of the captured defenders of Alençon in 1051/2 persuaded the garrison of nearby Domfront to surrender. Again in 1066 the destruction of Romney prompted the more important port of Dover to give up without a fight. But towards the end of his life William's use of terror became uncontrollable. While his relentless progress through southern England certainly convinced London to open its gates to the duke in December 1066, the ravaging of the North four years later was, he admitted, an atrocity 'beyond all reason'.[11]

Very little is known about William's mother, Herleve. She must have been a remarkable woman. Adelaide, her other illegitimate child, married well – and often – first Enguerrand, Count of Ponthieu, second Lambert of Lens, and finally Odo, Count of

Champagne. Herleve's children by Herluin had distinguished careers. The eldest, Odo, became Bishop of Bayeux and Duke of Kent, while the younger, Robert, was made Count Mortain. Both helped William regain Normandy, and conquer England, being amply rewarded for their services with lands and their half-brother's favour, until Odo's defection in 1088. That Herluin gave his second son, Robert, the same name as his wife's lover would suggest that he harboured no grudge against William's father, and might well have accorded the boy an honoured place in Herleve's new family. If – as seems reasonable to assume – her first-born was Herleve's favourite, then she would have endowed him with 'the feeling of a conqueror, that confidence of success that often induces real success' which Freud called 'the legacy of a mother's favour'.[12]

The legacy that his father left William was very different. No doting parent gave it to him; he had to seize it with the desperate vigour of his own determination.

Bastardy is a cruel rejection. Having had his pleasure a bastard's father refuses to do his duty, and by implication says that his child, and its mother, are not good enough for him. It has been argued that Robert would have married Herleve had she not been within the church's forbidden degree of blood relationship that prohibited unions between relatives as distant as third cousins. Yet marrying Herleve off to Herluin in about 1030 and suddenly deciding to leave his dukedom for a pilgrimage were the actions of an irresponsible young man who had no wish to settle down immediately into ducal domesticity. If William's reputed deathbed assertion that 'my father went into voluntary exile, entrusting me to the Duchy of Normandy' is an accurate version of what he said, it was also a deliberate distortion of the truth, which suggests that William both resented his father's desertion, being unable to admit to the real reason for Robert's departure, and at the same time wanted to believe that Robert had abdicated, and deeded him Normandy, rather than naming him heir just in case he failed to come home.[13]

William was extremely sensitive about the circumstances of his birth. After he captured the defenders of Alençon, who had taunted him by waving skins and hides from the castle wall in an insulting allusion to his grandfather's trade, William punished them, according to one story, by amputating all their limbs, or according to another, skinning them alive. At times he seemed to blame his illegitimacy for all his early troubles. 'Calling me a bastard, degenerate, and unworthy to reign,' he ruminated, Guy of Burgundy 'strove to strip

8 *William and his successors, William Rufus, Henry I and Stephen.* Each of the four kings holds a model of a church that they founded. The Normans formed an alliance with the Catholic church which they used to validate the legitimacy of their conquest

me of the whole of Normandy. Thus, while I was yet a beardless youth, I found myself compelled to . . . fight on the plain of Val-ès-Dunes.' A few years later, he continued, his uncles Mauger and William 'treated me with contempt as a bastard' by persuading Henry I, King of France, and Enguerrand, his brother-in-law, to invade Normandy.[14]

Uncertain of his birth, William insisted on the certainty of his rule. 'Normandy is mine by hereditary descent,' he told his eldest son, whom he christened Robert, as if to underscore the legitimacy of continuous succession.[15] Just before the battle of Hastings William challenged Harold to trial by combat, telling his men that the Earl of Wessex 'will fight to retain what he has wrongfully seized, whereas we shall fight to regain what we have received as a gift, and what we have lawfully acquired'.[16] While the *Anglo-Saxon Chronicle* maintained that Harold had been crowned by Archbishop Ealdred of York, the Norman chroniclers assert that Archbishop Stigand of Canterbury conducted the service; because the pope had deprived Stigand of his office, they insinuated, the usurper's consecration was invalid.

Illegitimacy also implies breaking the promise of parenthood by failing to give the child what should rightfully be his. After his father left him Normandy, William recalled, 'my dearest friends, my own kindred' tried to take it from him. After Edward had left him England, and Harold had sworn to uphold the bequest, the faithless earl tried to steal it away. William saw himself as someone deprived, someone picked upon. His cause was always right – thus at the battle of Hastings he wore in a bag about his neck some of the relics upon which Harold had given his word.

In several ways William's own marriage to Matilda reflected his views on his parents' liaison. He was very loyal to his wife, wanting to postpone his coronation in Westminster Abbey until she could arrive in England to share his glory. He had no known love affairs, and an abhorrence of immorality, particularly among priests who could never marry and legitimize their progeny. William first proposed marriage to Count Baldwin's daughter in about 1047, and wed her several years later in defiance of the ban that Pope Leo IV issued at the Council of Rheims in October 1049. Although William gained much from becoming allied to Count Baldwin, ruler of a powerful fiefdom, particularly after 1060 when Baldwin became the King of France's guardian, at the time William was taking an uncharacteristic risk in scorning the order of the pope – a father figure – particularly as Leo probably issued it at the instigation of Henry I and the Holy Roman Emperor. William and Matilda were grateful enough when Lanfranc, Prior of Le Bec, negotiated a settlement with Pope Nicholas II in 1059 to found and endow a monastery and nunnery at Caen, and eventually made the prior Archbishop of Canterbury. By 1066, instead of defying the pope, William sent his chaplain Gilbert Maminot to Rome to convince him of 'the legitimate rights of the duke', and obtain the banner that William flew during the battle of Hastings signifying that the conquest had the Holy Father's blessing.[17]

Rome's endorsement notwithstanding, the invasion of England was an audacious leap in the dark that defied all common prudence. William was extremely lucky; for the experienced Harold made several bad errors. He should, for instance, never have rushed south from Stamford Bridge, leaving many of his troops behind, whilst tiring out the rest to force a battle in which he lacked the advantage of surprise. Instead Harold should have waited, contained the Normans, and let the onset of winter, internal feuds, and lack of supplies, wear the invaders down. The duke was, of course, an able and courageous leader, who realized that he must defeat the Anglo-Saxons as quickly and decisively as possible: but more dangerous than any cool-headed military appreciation of the situation was his hot-hearted conviction of the rightness of his cause. Up to 1066 William had been a cautious man. He had besieged Brionne Castle, one of the strongest in France, for three years before starving Guy of Burgundy into submission. In 1066 he could have remained the unchallenged master of Normandy, who might have taken advantage of minor rulers in France and Anjou to expand his territories. Instead he launched a seaborne invasion, against the prevailing winds, across a hundred miles of some of the stormiest seas in the world, upon a far larger nation ruled by an experienced warrior. Only a desperate man, compelled by some unquenchable inner need, would have staked all on such a reckless gamble.

This inner drive was the real legacy that Duke Robert left his bastard. The distinguished psychoanalyst Erik Erikson has observed that great men are frequently driven by some paternal curse with which they must live, and which they must live down.[18] For Luther it was his father's brutality, for Gandhi his father's death, for William parental rejection. Throughout his life William tried to compensate for early deprivation in several ways. He loved food, for instance. At the crisis of the invasion, as his ship was alone in the middle of the Channel, William ate a large banquet. During his later years he become so obese that the King of France said he had the belly of a pregnant woman, and in death his bloated corpse had to be forced into the coffin. Beneath all the courage and resolution, the cruelty and paranoia, prowled a deeper, more insatiable hunger. 'Into avarice he did fall,' lamented the *Anglo-Saxon Chronicle*, 'and loved greediness above all.' But most of all William loved power, and it was through conquest that he was best able to exorcise the curse of his youth.[19] 'I was', he confessed, as he lay dying in agony, 'bred to arms from my childhood, and am stained with the rivers of blood I have shed.'[20]

III

JOHN

Few monarchs have been so reviled as John – the first, and the last, of that most common Christian name to rule England. According to *1066 and All That*, the repository of public conceptions – or rather misconceptions – about history, John was 'a bad king' who 'had begun badly as a Bad Prince'. Contemporary opinion was just as sweeping. 'No man dare trust him', concluded the troubadour Bertran de Born, 'for his heart is soft and cowardly'.[1] Posterity has been even less kind. To the Victorians, John was a man of 'almost superhuman wickedness'.[2] They found the lecher who hounded husbands and fathers to pleasure himself with their wives and daughters as odious as the traitor who surrendered England as a fief to the Bishop of Rome. If they believed that English history was the story of enlightened progress towards that constitutional monarchy which Victoria epitomized, then Magna Carta, the first milestone on that happy journey, was as benevolent as the malignancy of the king who had been forced to concede it. No wonder one eminent Victorian concluded, 'Foul as it is hell is defouled by the fouler presence of John.'[3]

Less sure in their own moral judgments (as well, perhaps, as of those of the Almighty), modern historians have been more charitable. They have explained away the harsh verdicts of contemporary chroniclers as the natural bias of churchmen against the monarch whose realm the pope put under an interdict (which, in effect, meant that the church went on strike), and who threatened to hang the Archbishop of Canterbury the moment he laid hands on him. After ploughing through the runs of public records, which really start in his reign, modern historians have praised John's abilities as an administrator and judge. The loss of Normandy to the French in 1205 and the baronial revolt of 1215 were not really John's fault; they were the results of a rising tide of nationalism abroad, and aristocratic selfishness at home, which in their turn were the inevitable reaction to nearly a century of strong Angevin rule.

And so the superhumanly wicked John has become, to quote the title of a recent biography, 'The Maligned Monarch'.[4]

At one level this metamorphosis may be explained quite simply: since the Victorian era sexual promiscuity has become personal fulfilment; toadying to Rome, ecumenicalism; that John 'feared not God', irrelevant, when He is widely presumed dead; losing a duchy in France, forgivable – even laudable – for a generation that has lost a worldwide empire; being a diligent administrator and jurist, worthy, at a time that has seen an explosive growth in the number and influence of lawyers and bureaucrats.[5] Not surprisingly the records that historians have used have biased their conclusions. Medieval clerical chronicles condemned the king just as understandably as his own court records praise him. Neither really come to terms with the true nature of his personality, and thus of his reign. The answer to these questions may, therefore, lie in his childhood, where the king's character, like all men's, was indelibly shaped.

John was born on Christmas Eve 1166, a hundred years, less a day, after his great-great-grandfather William the Conqueror had been crowned in Westminster Abbey. Over the past century the monarchy had become increasingly secure, greatly expanding its authority to bring stability to its ever-growing dominions. His parents' marriage was, however, anything but stable. Soon after John was born they separated. His father, Henry II, took Rosamund Clifford as his mistress, having two sons by her. Later, when Eleanor plotted against him, the King kept her imprisoned in Winchester Castle for sixteen years.

Eleanor of Aquitaine was one of those remarkable women who have been able to stamp their personalities upon history. Duchess of Aquitaine in her own right, she married Louis VII of France when she was fifteen. Although they had two daughters, their relationship was far from satisfying. He became moody and monkish; she devoted herself to courtly love and the poetry of the troubadours. After he suspected that she had failed to live up to her platonic ideals with some of his friends during a crusade, he had their marriage annulled in 1152. Eleanor promptly remarried Henry of Anjou, eleven years her junior, who two years later inherited the English throne. They had eight children, John their youngest being born when his mother was forty-five and his father thirty-four.

Perhaps the difference of their ages, or else the clash of two strong personalities, destroyed Henry and Eleanor's marriage. Cast aside for a younger woman, she certainly became bitter, reputedly telling

John the legend that his father's family, the Angevins, were all descended from the devil.

No one could deny that Henry had a frantic energy that could, at times, erupt into almost demonic rages, as when he ordered the murder of Thomas à Becket. With vigour and skill he ruled a vast empire stretching, he liked to boast, from the Pyrenees to the Arctic Ocean. Although John was his favourite child, Henry ultimately fell out with him, being unable to accept his sons' coming of age. This was ironic, for Henry spent much time and effort trying to devise inheritances for them. He failed, and broke with his sons as bitterly as he had with their mother.

At first Henry tried to side-step the problem with John by placing him when just over a year old in the care of the Abbey of Fontevrault in Anjou. He hoped that the monks would bring him up to enter the church, and that (like the king's illegitimate son, Geoffrey) he would become a bishop and so have no need of an inheritance to support a family. But John came to hate the abbey so much that his father had to remove him to the household of his eldest brother, Henry. Here the young prince learned the chivalric arts of hunting, jousting, and may even have had Ranulf Glanville, the king's highly competent justiciar, as his tutor. When Henry fell ill at La Motte-de-Ger, and thought he was dying, he bequeathed John's guardian-ship to Prince Henry (and not Eleanor), with the request that the eight-month-old infant be made Duke of Mortain, the venerable honour held by a junior member of the Norman ducal family. But when Henry recovered, he promptly forgot his request.

The king's omission reveals the ambivalence he felt towards all his sons. While he wanted to give them love, and even his lands, he could not bring himself to do so gracefully and without hesitation. When they were young he liked his children to stay at his court as it moved from castle to castle, particularly during the Christmas season, but he never provided them with the stable and settled home essential for a child's healthy development. Henry, however, was more concerned with his children's financial than their emotional security. Even before John's birth, he had promised England to his eldest son, Henry, the Young King (crowned in his father's lifetime as a precaution); Aquitaine to his second son, Richard; and Brittany, to his third legitimate son, Geoffrey. So nothing was left for the youngest son, who may well have been a mistake, engendered by one last desperate physical coupling to save a doomed marriage.

9 *Fourteenth-century miniature depicting John out hunting.* Although charming, this suggests that weak slyness which contemporaries recognized, particularly when they compared John to his parents, or his brother Richard

10 *Henry II silver penny,* minted by Gordon of Worcester. Though artistically crude, this image conveys something of the determination and ferocity of a monarch who not only fought with his wife Eleanor of Aquitaine and Archbishop Thomas à Becket, but fell out with all four of his legitimate sons. The defection of his youngest and favourite son, John, who rebelled against him in 1189, hastened Henry II's death

Henry certainly recognized his last child's dilemma by cruelly nick-naming him John 'Lackland'.

To remedy the situation, in 1181 Henry tried to marry John to Alice, the eldest daughter of the Count of Maurienne, in the hope that eventually the twelve-year-old boy would inherit that pros-perous fief in northwest Italy. When the count inquired what Henry intended giving his son in return, unthinkingly he replied Chinon, Loudon and Mirabeau castles. These had already been promised to the Young King, who was so upset that with his mother's help he rebelled against his father. It took Henry two years to crush the rebellion, by which time Alice of Maurienne had died, as had John's expectations. So in paltry compensation for the loss of a virtually independent principality Henry betrothed John to Isabella, the Earl of Gloucester's daughter.

Two months after the Young King's death in June 1183, Henry ordered John and Ranulf Glanville to leave England to join him and Richard in Normandy. He asked Richard to concede his claim to Aquitaine in return for the Young King's to England and Normandy. Richard refused. Although England and Normandy were far larger than Aquitaine, Richard had enjoyed much more independence from his father in Aquitaine than had his elder brother. Rather than insisting that Richard obey, the king was untypically indecisive. A year later he returned to England after, so the story goes, advising John to 'lead an army into Richard's territories and win them for himself by force'.[6] John and Geoffrey (a malevolent influence if ever there was one) raised troops and invaded Poitou, burning and pillaging, and Richard retaliated by wreaking similar havoc on the equally innocent peasantry of Brittany. Realizing that things had got out of control Henry ordered his sons to England, where in December he made them sign the Peace of Westminster, from which, once again, John got nothing.

The following year the Patriarch of Jerusalem came to England with what must have seemed to the much-thwarted John an offer he could hardly refuse: Baldwin IV, King of Jerusalem, and a member of a cadet Angevin line, was dying of leprosy, and being childless desperately needed to adopt an heir.[7] Further investigation revealed that Baldwin's offer was not as appealing as the patriarch had led the king to believe. The King of Jerusalem had little real authority, affairs there being extraordinarily chaotic, and if John was to be anything more than a king in title, Henry would have to fight an expensive and uncertain war thousands of miles from home. So in a carefully orchestrated meeting at Clerkenwell the king asked his council for their advice. Together they opposed the scheme. Even though John went down on his knees and begged his father to give him a patrimony in the Middle East, Henry refused. His plans for the boy's future lay far closer to home.

It is one of the ironies of Anglo-Irish history that England's involvement with Ireland began with a grant from the pope – albeit an English pope, Adrian IV. In about 1156 he sent Henry II the bull *De Laudabiliter* authorizing him to colonize Ireland. In 1171 Henry invaded the country and within six months established his personal authority there. Once planted in Ireland's stony soil, however, English hegemony soon withered away. Half a dozen years later Henry let it be known that he had not forsaken his effort to control Ireland, by announcing that he eventually intended to give it to John. Thus in 1185, after knighting the seventeen-year-old boy at Windsor Castle, Henry sent him to Ireland with sixty ships, three hundred knights, numerous archers and a generous baggage train. According to the chronicler Gerald of Wales, John bungled the venture from the moment he landed. He and his foppish cronies mocked the Irish chieftains who had come to welcome them, laughing at their clothes and pulling their long beards, both having long since gone out of fashion in England. The humiliated chiefs complained to the kings and princes of Connaught and Munster, who refused to attend John's court in Dublin. Here John wasted the silver intended for his soldiers' pay in riotous living, forcing the men to plunder, mutiny and eventually desert. John too deserted, suddenly running home in September; his first independent command had turned into complete and utter humiliation.

Although Henry II was not as critical of John's behaviour as posterity has been, and indeed made further plans to place his son on the Irish throne, John was far from grateful. So after Geoffrey died in 1186, fatally wounded in a tournament, the king intensified his policy of playing his remaining two legitimate sons against each other, once threatening Richard that he would leave all his dominions to John. But Henry failed to either divide or rule. By 1189 the king had driven John into a secret alliance with Richard, who with secret aid from the King of France, Philip Augustus, was fighting Henry II. On 4 July they forced Henry, who was dying, to accept their terms. In return they gave him a list of all their allies, open and covert. 'Can it be true,' exclaimed the king, as Geoffrey, Archbishop of York (his bastard, yet only faithful son), read out the first name,

11 *Statue of Richard I*, by Marochetti, 1861, outside the Houses of Parliament. This Victorian image of Richard shows the crusader king of legend, Coeur de Lion. Even though John usurped his authority when Richard was away on crusade, the king cuttingly dismissed this treachery as the solecism of a silly boy who could not have known better

12 *Carved capital from the church of Notre-Dame-du-Bourg*, Langon, near Bordeaux, believed to depict Henry II and Eleanor of Aquitaine. John's mother was a formidable woman whose stormy relations with her husband had a malign effect on her youngest son's childhood

13 *John and Philip Augustus*. Although this fourteenth-century illuminated manuscript depicts the two kings exchanging a kiss of peace, in fact they devoted most of their energies to fighting a war. It resulted in the loss of considerable English territory in France, and the constitutional crisis that culminated in the sealing of Magna Carta 'that John, my heart, whom I have loved more than all my other sons, has forsaken me? Read no more. I care no more for myself or this world.' Two days later Henry died, his last words being, 'Shame, shame on a vanquished king.'[7]

The new reign started as inauspiciously as the old one ended. During Richard's coronation a crazed bat flew about Westminster Abbey. When the king leaned on the white pilgrims' staff, the symbol given to all who promised to go on a crusade, it snapped. It is no surprise, therefore, that just before he left England in 1189 Richard tried to prevent his younger brother from usurping power by designating his nephew, Arthur of Brittany, his successor, appointing William Longchamp regent, and making John promise not to enter England for at least three years, by which time Richard was sure he would be home, a hero back from the wars.

But it did not work out that way. John broke his promise, came back to England and deposed Longchamp. Richard failed to capture Jerusalem, and on his way home was taken prisoner by the Holy Roman Emperor. Despite the machinations of John and Philip Augustus, the ransom money was raised, and in 1194, after a five-year absence, Richard returned to his dominions, much to John's trepidation. 'Tell him to come to me without fear, he is my brother,' promised the king. 'I will not hold his folly against him.' When John emerged from hiding and threw himself trembling at his brother's feet to beg forgiveness, the king kept his word. Raising him, Richard dismissed his treachery with humiliating condescension: 'Think no more of it, John. You are only a child.'

And thus in May 1194, when John was twenty-six, in a very real sense his much-prolonged childhood ended. John became his brother's loyal lieutenant, developing the administrative and legal skills that were to flower after he inherited the throne in 1199. But although John seemed to have learned his lesson and to have become more mature, the fatal defects of character engendered in his earliest years remained just below the surface.

Contemporaries had a very poor opinion of Prince John's character. Robert of Auxerre called him 'a feckless young man, who takes things easy'. William of Newburgh thought he was 'a very foolish youth'.[8] Gerald of Wales described the twenty-year-old prince as 'caught in the toils and snared by the temptations of unstable and dissolute youth, he was as wax to receive impressions of evil, but hardened against those who would have warned him of its danger; compliant to the fancy of the moment; making no resistance to the impulses of nature; more given to luxurious ease than to warlike exercises, to enjoyment than to endurance, to vanity than to virtue'.[9]

Gerald's description, the only one from a chronicler who knew John personally, hints at two seemingly contradictory facets of his personality. First, John was driven by some inner storm, some frantic energy, which may have come from the deep feelings of insecurity that he tried to mask by playing the fop. Secondly, he was an extraordinarily ambitious man, held back by few personal restraints, determined not to be outclassed by his father either as an administrator or as a judge – skills that John valued far more than his bellicose barons. In sum 'he had the mental abilities of a great king, but the inclinations of a petty tyrant'.[10]

Like Richard, John inherited considerable energy from his father. During the whole of his reign he only once stayed in a place for longer than thirty days, and that was to besiege Rochester Castle. Constantly travelling about his lands, John hunted his way across England, dispensing justice in some county town, before riding to London, collecting taxes along the way, to preside over a meeting of the Exchequer. Sometimes John exploded into uncontrollable rages. Just as his father had lost his temper with Archbishop Becket, so John stormed at Chancellor Longchamp. 'His whole person became so changed as to be hardly recognizable,' one witness recalled. 'Rage contorted his brow, his burning eyes glittered, bluish spots discoloured the pink of his cheek.' Even though John learned to control his emotions as he grew older, he never tamed them. In 1203 he murdered his nephew, Arthur of Brittany, in a drunken rage, throwing the weighted corpse in the Seine, and eight years later at Nottingham he needlessly hanged twenty-eight Welsh hostages.

John's rages were both a psychological and a genetic legacy from his father. As Gerald of Wales recalled, on his sons Henry 'lavished in their childhood more than a father's affection, but in their more advanced years he looked askance at them after the manner of a stepfather'.[11] Split between giving his sons inheritances and trying to retain control of his realms, Henry did neither, and alienated his boys as bitterly as he had their mother. They identified with Eleanor. Richard did so to such a degree that he was rumoured to be a homosexual. John protected his mother in her old age. In 1202 in an uncharacteristically decisive military move he captured Mirabeau, where rebels had trapped his mother in the castle keep, freeing her from prison, as he had been unable to do when his father had locked

14 *Effigy of John on his tomb in Worcester Cathedral.* Just before his death ended the civil war, John ordered that he be buried in the cathedral. This effigy, executed twenty years afterwards, is the best likeness we have of this troubled monarch

her up so he could enjoy his mistresses undisturbed.

From his mother John may have received his feckless cunning. She was 'a very clever woman, born of noble stock,' recorded a contemporary, 'but flighty'.[12] Unlike her son, however, she had a steely self-confidence and sense of purpose. As a child, John never knew his mother, neither did he find a substitute, such as a nurse or nanny, to give him that 'feeling of a conqueror' which William I enjoyed. Instead, his parents' bitter quarrels left him with a sense of guilt, of being somehow to blame, of being forced to choose sides – feelings which are all too common among children who have been through a divorce. Worse still, his father not only tried to play his children off against their mother, but against each other. Constantly he promised John some inheritance, only to withhold it, until finally John turned against his father in an attempt to seize it for himself. A lack of land, an inability to secure financial independence, or even to find some widely accepted adult skill such as military prowess, unduly prolonged John's adolescence, making him even more insecure.

To a mean nature John added grandiose ambitions. He wanted to build as large an empire as had his father, wherein he could exercise his considerable administrative talents. He may have learned them from Ranulf Glanville, Henry's highly competent minister, who was perhaps closer to the young John than was his real father. The two travelled together. John may have spent most of his formative years in Ranulf's household, where many of the young knights who accompanied him on the Irish expedition grew up.

When a contemporary wrote that John 'was a great prince, but hardly a happy one', he sensed the contradictory nature of the king's character which revealed itself in a number of ways.[13] The one that most offended John's subjects was his open lack of religion. Far worse than his quarrel with the pope, or (as was widely, although wrongly, believed) his crushing to death of Geoffrey, Archdeacon of Norwich, under a cope of lead, was John's blatant agnosticism – a rare yet perilous commodity in the Middle Ages.[14] 'You happy beast – never forced to prattle prayers, nor dragged to the Sacrament,' he reportedly told a dead buck at the end of a day's hunt – a sport he loved as flagrantly as he had despised religion ever since his unhappy infancy at Fontevrault Abbey.[15]

Nearly as offensive as his reputation as an unbeliever was his reputation as a philanderer. Of course, generous sexual appetites were nothing new in the English royal family: Henry II acknowledged three bastards, Henry I at least twenty-one. But John was attracted to the wives and daughters of the high-born. Many believed that just because Robert FitzWalter's daughter refused to sleep with him he razed her father's castle, drove him into exile, and had her poisoned. Others were convinced that John's propositioning of Eustace de Vesci's wife made the two men bitter enemies, Eustace being one of the leaders of the baronial revolt that culminated in Magna Carta.

John sealed the charter not because he recognized its constitutional significance (no one else did at the time), nor because he intended keeping its terms, but in order to avoid a confrontation. As the youngest child of a bitterly fragmented family, constantly dependent on the good will of others, far more powerful than he, for any hope of preferment, John learned not to alienate those above him. He merged into the background, avoiding issues, passively hoping for the best. This characteristic was readily apparent during the Irish expedition. He left Dublin for home suddenly in September 1185 not because he had caroused enough with his friends and drunk all his soldiers' pay, but because he could not face a conflict with the native Irish. Ironically the administrators he left behind, John Comyn, Bertram de Verdon, and Gilbert Pipard managed to do so well that effective English hegemony in the Pale dates from John's youthful invasion.[16] Again John lost Normandy in 1205 mainly because he could not bring himself to act decisively to relieve Château Gaillard, the strategically placed castle on the river Seine above Rouen, which was the key to the whole duchy. Indeed, the day that Philip Augustus took Château Gaillard, John was safely in England, ordering that wild beasts be trapped to ensure good hunting that summer in the New Forest.

John's reluctance to face problems appeared – particularly to those he let down – as untrustworthiness. He had a pettiness of spirit that made him, one chronicler recorded, 'almost as many enemies as barons'. As a result of his earliest years he saw the world belonging to two very distinct groups. 'It is only reasonable that we should do better by those that are with us than those who are against us,' John once admitted.[17] But he did far worse to his enemies, who were legion, than for his friends, who became ever fewer. With his own hands he murdered Arthur, his nephew, whose claim to the throne was just as good as his. He executed the Welsh hostages in a fit of pique, and supposedly starved to death William de Briouze's wife and children in a needless act of revenge.

Untrusted, John could not trust other people. He became so concerned about what was said of him at court that he made his courtiers promise to report 'if they hear anything hostile to the Lord King'. He devised such complicated procedures for the interrogation of prisoners, that he sometimes forgot whom he had asked to do what to whom. No wonder the barons tried to pin him down in Magna Carta, which was less the cornerstone of the constitution than a paperweight designed to prevent an extraordinarily slippery feudal lord from slithering out from under his obligations. It failed on every count. Months after the sealing of the Great Charter civil war broke out in England, the French invaded, and only John's death in October 1216 ended hostilities. That John passed away from eating too many eels was an apt coincidence, for those snake-like creatures ended a flawed reign that, in spite of John's undoubted administrative and juristic abilities, was, the chroniclers quite rightly observed, the product of a fractured childhood. As his reign revealed, John as a child lacked far more than land.

IV

HENRY VIII

No king has captured and retained the public's imagination as completely as Henry VIII. In this century, for instance, films have portrayed him as a Rabelaisian figure of gross proportions and grosser appetites, brawling, belching, and bawdying his way through countless feasts, six wives and one Reformation. Many contemporaries agreed with Hollywood. 'The King of England, this Henry, clearly lies, and with his lies acts more the part of a comic jester than that of a king', lamented Martin Luther. 'He is a wonderful man, and has wonderful people about him,' thought the French ambassador, 'but is a sly old fox.' Others – particularly subjects whose necks were protected neither by distance nor by diplomatic immunity – were more generous. Soon after Henry came to the throne Lord Mountjoy wrote to his dear friend Erasmus, 'if you could see how all the world here is rejoicing in the accession of so great a prince, you could not contain your tears of joy. The heavens laugh, the earth exults, all things are full of milk, of honey and of nectar. Avarice is expelled the earth. Liberality scatters wealth with bounteous hand. Our king does not desire gold, or gems, or precious stones, but virtue, glory and immortality.'[1]

Of his first two desires Henry found little. He displayed scant virtue in marrying six wives, divorcing a couple and executing two more. He won even less glory with a series of useless and expensive military campaigns against the French and Scots. And yet he has gained a degree of immortality unsurpassed by any other English monarch. Far from diminishing the impact of his character the passage of time has caricatured it, bringing out the strange combination of insecurity and egomania that forced through the break with Rome, and the ensuing changes in religion, government and parliament that made his reign one of the most significant in English history.

Henry's personality was so confusing that one medical man has

15 *Margaret Beaufort, Countess of Richmond and Derby,* statue from her tomb by Torrigiano. Henry spent a happy childhood in the care of his maternal grandmother, a remarkable woman who educated him in the new learning of humanism

called him 'a Jekyll and Hyde', whilst another has diagnosed the king as 'a psychopath of the boasting, swaggering, self-maintaining and self-glorying type'.[2] He could be magnanimously open, and then sullenly secretive. He was both charismatic and repellent, generous and selfish, a virile swain and a cuckold seemingly unable to satisfy a young wife. One day he would reward a trusted servant with yet another lucrative sinecure, and the next box his ears. Being lazy he came to depend on his ministers; being insecure he resented surrendering power to them; being energetic he liked to retain final control in his own hand – three contradictions that ended in his ministers' ruin and their master's remorse. Henry was a tyrant with a profound respect for the law. No matter how many and how odious were the crimes he committed, the king insisted that they be done legally. Thus he ordered parliament to pass a statute making him in effect an emperor independent of all outside authority, at the same time as he desperately wanted that authority – the pope – to approve his divorce. He was learned and scholarly. He revered the wisdom of the past, and yet destroyed a millenium of English Roman Catholic Christendom. He wrote a book defending the pope's prerogatives, and a decade later expelled the Bishop of Rome forever from England. Women both repelled and attracted Henry. He first loved Anne Boleyn so passionately that he was prepared to defy the Catholic church, and then hated her so implacably that he sent her to the block. As a father Henry was equally contradictory. He accepted and rejected his daughters, Mary and Elizabeth, so completely and capriciously that he inflicted upon them as children and adolescents many of the wounds he had suffered in his early life.

Henry VIII was born at Greenwich Palace on 28 June 1491, and christened a few days later by Richard Foxe, Bishop of Exeter, in the nearby church of the Observant Franciscans, the font having been specially brought from Canterbury Cathedral. Little is known about his earliest years. He was a healthy, red-headed, strong-limbed baby, who was fond enough of his nurse, Anne Luke, to pay her a generous £20 per annum pension when he became king. His miserly father, Henry Tudor, King Henry VII, gave his second son several offices of state, less for their honour, than for their income. He made him Lord Warden of the Cinque Ports in April 1492, and Lord Lieutenant of Ireland and Warden of the Scottish Marches the following year. That October the king ordered his second son brought from Eltham Palace, some eight miles southeast of the capital, to Westminster, where before the entire court, the Lord Mayor and Aldermen of London, and both houses of parliament, he made him Duke of Cornwall. The next year Henry Tudor made his son a Knight of the Garter. In September 1496, at the age of five, the prince performed his first public duty by witnessing the charter granted to the Abbot and Convent of Glastonbury. Two years later he rode in great state into London, the streets having been specially swept for the occasion, to receive a gift from the city, for which he gave his first recorded speech of thanks.

While such public events captured the notice of chroniclers ever interested in the ceremony of royalty, the private details of Henry's early childhood have passed almost unnoticed. It seems to have been happy enough. Henry was especially fond of his younger sister, Margaret, enjoyed his studies, and, if Erasmus is to be believed, was a disturbingly precocious young lad. One day in 1499, Erasmus recalled two decades later, he and Thomas More walked over from Lord Mountjoy's house to Eltham to see the royal children. Henry was patiently doing his lessons surrounded by his admiring sisters Mary and Margaret and his baby brother Edmund. Erasmus thought that the prince had 'already something of royalty in his demeanour, in which there was a certain dignity combined with singular courtesy'. More gave the boy some Latin verses he had written specially, and that evening Erasmus received a request from Henry for a similar tribute. The great humanist (who at a pinch could turn out a monograph in just over a week) was so perturbed (and not a little annoyed with More), that it took him three days to pen some suitable lines.[3] As early as the age of eight Henry knew how to discomfit men far greater than himself.

Perhaps he owed this to his mother's lack and his grandmother's excess of influence on his childhood. His mother, Elizabeth of York, the daughter of Edward IV, was a passive woman whose ability to live in what More called 'peaceable accord' with her husband and her formidable mother-in-law resulted mainly from allowing the two to do pretty well what they pleased. Henry Tudor's mother, Lady Margaret Beaufort, controlled her grandchildren's education as efficiently as she founded chairs and colleges at Cambridge University.

Others too played a part in Henry's education. Bernard André taught him history by writing his life of Henry Tudor. Giles D'Ewes, a noted grammarian and amateur alchemist, instructed him in French. He may have studied mathematics, geometry and

16 *Arthur, Prince of Wales*, artist unknown. As the heir to the throne, Arthur was a popular and commanding figure. He was far too grand to have much to do with his younger brother, who lived for much of his childhood under his shadow

17 *Henry VII*, 1505, by Michiel Sittow. Painted to further the marriage negotiations between the widowed king and Margaret, daughter of the Emperor Maximilian (and thus presumably intended to show Henry VII at his best), this portrait none the less reveals an intensely cold man astronomy with Thomas More. The man who had most influence over the prince's education, however, was John Skelton, a skilled poet and a protégé of Margaret Beaufort, who was his chief tutor from 1495 to 1502.

> *The honour of England I learned to spell*
> *In dignity royal that doth excel.*
> *I gave him drink of the sugared well.*

So Skelton boasted twenty years later. Without doubt the poet fostered Henry's musical talents, having him taught to play the lute, organ and virginals, to sight read fluently, to sing well, and to compose works which are still sung today. He awakened his pupil's love of theology, with its fierce arguments over arcane details that Henry seemed to relish during the long and complex debate over his divorce, and the subsequent religious changes. He taught the boy to speak and write several languages, his Latin being so fluent that Cardinal Bainbridge once told Henry that no other prince drafted such eloquent diplomatic dispatches. In all, Skelton produced a well-educated young man with a zest for scholarship, who on becoming king confessed to More that he wished he was more learned. Skelton was genuinely fond of his pupil – a sentiment the tutor evinced for few of his fellow creatures – calling the lad 'a delightful small new rose, worthy of its stock'. For Henry's edification he wrote *Speculum Principis*, a ponderous advice book that counselled the boy not to rely too much on ministers and to 'choose a wife for yourself, prize her always and uniquely'. None the less, as Henry's wives and ministers could later have testified, Skelton was not an entirely effective teacher, for basically he was a quarrelsome, morose man of uncontrollable temper, who exacerbated the contradictory parts of his charge's character.

For the first decade of Henry's life his upbringing did not matter too much, for as a second son he counted for little, being expected to play second fiddle to his elder brother, Arthur, Prince of Wales. It was in this secondary capacity that his father sent him in November 1501 to Kingston-upon-Thames to welcome to England Arthur's fiancée, Catherine of Aragon, the daughter of Ferdinand and Isabella. He escorted her to the Archbishop of Canterbury's palace at Lambeth, and the next day they processed through the city. At her marriage a few days later he walked the bride up the aisle of St Paul's Cathedral, and afterwards he danced at the wedding breakfast, to the delight of all who saw him throw off his coat so as to be better able to lead the festivities.

Arthur and Catherine's joy was not to last. Henry Tudor sent the Prince and Princess of Wales to Ludlow, where four months later Arthur died suddenly of consumption, leaving Catherine a widow at sixteen, and Henry heir to the throne.

Eleven months later, on 2 February 1503, Henry suffered a second loss when his mother died giving birth to a premature daughter, who followed her to the grave a few weeks afterwards. Although some four years later Henry wrote to Erasmus that 'never since the death of my dearest mother hath there come to me more hateful intelligence' than that of the demise of the King of Castile, it seems that he wrote more from convention than out of genuine anguish.[4] Henry had never been close to his mother, experiencing a far greater sense of bereavement when his favourite sister, Margaret, left England in 1503 after marrying James IV of Scotland.

After Arthur's death Henry Tudor had no intention of improving his son's position, which if anything grew worse. He did not give the boy any state papers to read, nor teach him the art of kingship. Neither did he send him off to the relative independence of Ludlow, to help rule the principality of Wales, preferring to keep him under his thumb in London. It was said that he confined the boy in a chamber which could only be reached through his own bedroom, so as to prevent the Spanish from inveigling him into a marriage alliance with Catherine of Aragon.

It was not that Henry Tudor disliked the young widow personally. Indeed, for a time he toyed with the idea of marrying her himself, being loath to return the instalment of the dowry paid on her marriage to Arthur. This probably explains why he agreed to Henry and Catherine's betrothal on 23 June 1503, on the condition that they marry in three years' time when the groom was fifteen and the bride four years his senior. But in June 1505, Henry Tudor made his son publicly renounce the marriage treaty, perhaps to pressure Catherine's father into paying the rest of the dowry, or else to further a new diplomatic initiative for the hand of Eleanor, daughter of Philip of Castile. Yet in October 1505 the pope wrote to Catherine telling her – at her fiancé's request – to look after her health in anticipation of their forthcoming marriage, and in April of the following year in a letter to Philip of Castile Henry described Catherine as 'my most dear and well beloved consort, the Princess, my wife'.[5]

While all these confused and confusing signals certainly bear the hallmarks of Henry Tudor's devious mind, it is hard to say what effect they had on his adolescent son. He seemed remarkably pliant. His only recorded protest against his father's schemes was when the king announced that he was thinking of marrying Joanna, Philip of Castile's widow. Henry objected that his father was too old, and Joanna too mad – she insisted on taking her late husband in his coffin with her wherever she went. Stung by his son's uncharacteristic independence and painful honesty, Henry Tudor 'scolded the prince, as though he would kill him', frightening him so badly that, according to the Spanish ambassador, he never again mentioned foreign affairs without his father's permission.

Henry's relations with his father confused diplomatic reporters. 'It is quite wonderful how much the king likes the Prince of Wales,' reported the Duke of Estrado; 'he wishes to improve him . . . nothing escapes his attention.'[6] But whatever the precise nature of their relationship, many observers agreed that the most important influence on the young prince was the old king. Henry proved as much when he came to the throne. On the second day of his reign he rejected decades of financial prudence by having Richard Empson and Edmund Dudley, his father's assiduous tax collectors, arrested on trumped-up charges of extortion and thrown into the Tower, where they languished for nineteen months before their heads were cut off. In the second month of his reign Henry VIII brushed aside a decade of parental procrastination by finally marrying Catherine, with whom he fell deeply and obviously in love.

After years of toying with his son's future it seems certain that the dying king told Henry to decide for himself whether or not to wed Catherine. Yet immediately after marrying her Henry VIII convinced others – as well as himself – that he had only done so out of filial devotion. In June 1509 he wrote to Mary of Savoy that 'on our coming of age, among other wise and honourable advice given to us by the king on his dying bed, was an express command to take the Lady Catherine to wife'.[7]

The young couple seemed to epitomize hope, pleasure, and self-confidence. Even though Henry credited his blissful marriage to his father's commands, their lifestyle exhibited an extravagance that blatantly contradicted Henry Tudor's notorious parsimony, and reached its peak at the Field of the Cloth of Gold, where in 1520 Henry VIII tried to outdo his rival, Francis I of France, in conspicuous consumption. As her portrait (Plate 19) shows,

Catherine was a strikingly attractive young woman. 'There is nothing wanting in her,' wrote Thomas More after seeing the princess ride through London, 'that the most beautiful girl should have.' Her husband was just as pleasing to the eye. 'The king is the handsomest potenate I ever set eyes upon,' one diplomat reported home.[8] 'His limbs are of gigantic size,' wrote another, 'of visage lovely, of body mighty strong.' He loved music, scouring the realm for boys to sing in his choir, for as he declared in a song he wrote at the time, 'youth will needs have dalliance'. He enjoyed hunting and hawking. He ran well, shot accurately, and swam with vigour. He rode at the tilt competing for Catherine's favours like the knight of old he longed to be.

But substitutes such as riding, hunting, and jousting for trinkets were not enough. Henry longed for war, and the glory that only battle could bring. As the Venetian ambassador noted, 'the new king is magnificent and a great enemy of the French'.[9] Henry himself confessed that it was 'his duty to seek fame by military skill', because he wanted to 'create such a fine opinion about his valour among all men that they would clearly understand that his ambition was not merely to equal but indeed to excel the glorious deeds of his ancestors'. Thus he sent an expeditionary force under the Marquees of Dorset to Gascony in 1513, and the following year personally led an invasion of northern France. In part his education prompted such ambitions. According to Erasmus, Henry's 'dream as a child had been the recovery of his French provinces'. As a boy he had read of his ancestors' noble achievements in Froissart's Chronicles, and on becoming king he promptly commissioned Lord Berners to translate them into English. Henry's thirst for glory came from a strange combination of good looks, talent, and popularity mixed with a fundamental sense of insecurity derived from his feelings about his father's military reputation. As Henry admitted in the course of a long conversation with More in 1522, he wanted to conquer France in order to eclipse Henry Tudor's victory over Richard III.[10]

Before Henry Tudor won the battle of Bosworth Field in August 1485 few Englishmen had thought he had any chance of winning the throne; afterwards not many more would have laid good odds on his retaining it. Born in Pembroke Castle in January 1457 Henry was the posthumous child of Edmund Tudor, Earl of Richmond, who had died three months earlier, leaving his wife, Margaret Beaufort, a widow at the age of thirteen. Henry Tudor's origins were obscure. His paternal great-grandfather had been an outlawed Welsh

18 *Henry VIII*, about 1520, aged twenty-nine, artist unknown. In his youth Henry's strength and virility, his intellectual and musical capacities, greatly impressed his subjects

19 *Catherine of Aragon*, about 1501, by Michiel Sittow. Painted just before her marriage to Arthur this portrait conveys some of the demure beauty that persuaded Henry to marry his brother's widow in 1509. As she aged, and failed to provide a male heir, Henry's eye lighted on Anne Boleyn (Plate 22)

brewer. His grandfather Owen Tudor had formed an illicit (and treasonable) liaison with Catherine of Valois, Henry V's widow, so secret that not until the birth of their fifth child did the council order them to separate. Henry's tenuous claim to the throne was through his mother's family, the Beauforts: his great grandfather was the belatedly legitimized son of John of Gaunt and Catherine Swynford, and so Henry was descended from King Edward III. Since during those dangerous days of the Wars of the Roses a drop of royal blood was enough to sign one's death warrant, particularly after the Yorkist victory at Tewkesbury in 1471, Henry Tudor, the last surviving male of the House of Lancaster, had to flee into exile in Brittany. A dozen years later, in 1483, he tried to return to England, but was driven away by the Dorset militia at Poole harbour. In 1485 a second invasion was more successful. The Welsh welcomed Henry Tudor when he landed at Milford Haven on 8 August 1485, marching under his banner, Cadwallader's red dragon, to Bosworth Field, where they routed the king's forces on the 22nd. During the battle Richard III was slain. Afterwards his corpse, stripped naked, a halter round its neck, was thrown across a pack horse, and, with its blood-matted hair dragging along the ground, was taken to Leicester, where after being exposed to public gaze for two days, it was tossed without ceremony into a grave in Gray Friar's Chapel.

Quite naturally the victor wished to avoid the vanquished's ignominious end. So in January 1486 Henry Tudor married Elizabeth, Edward IV's daughter, and thus united the houses of York and Lancaster. But this did not prevent challenges against his rule. Henry Tudor had to suppress the Lovell rebellion in 1486, the Lambert Simnel conspiracy in 1487, Perkin Warbeck's invasion of 1491, and the Earl of Suffolk's conspiracies a decade later. So his children grew up in a world of threats, intrigue, and paranoia. On the day that Henry was born his father was away preparing to repulse a French invasion. When he was six he and his mother had to flee to the safety of the Tower to escape a horde of Cornish peasants marching on the capital. All this taught him to be careful. As the Spanish ambassador Dr Rodrigo de Puebla recognized in 1508, Prince Henry 'is as prudent as to be expected from a son of Henry VII'.[11] But if Henry VIII inherited his caution and suspicion from his father, he lacked the latter's droll sense of proportion. Unlike Henry Tudor, Henry VIII could never have pardoned Lambert Simnel for being duped into impersonating Edward V, one of the princes Richard III was reputed to have murdered in the Tower, by making the lad a turnspit in the royal kitchens. Far from being able to forgive his enemies, Henry VIII often turned on his friends.

Henry's earliest years were as emotionally insecure as his father's reign was politically uncertain. At Christmas 1497 Sheen Palace burnt down, forcing the royal family to flee into the December cold to watch the flames consume their possessions. Well over half of Henry's siblings died before his twelfth birthday: Elizabeth in 1495, Edmund in 1500, Arthur in 1502, and an infant sister in 1503, the latter's birth being so difficult that it killed his mother. But rather than trying to heal such losses, Henry Tudor made them worse by bullying his son, callously dangling a series of marriage alliances before him, and all the time keeping a very tight rein on his behaviour and movements. In fact he kept his son 'as locked away as a woman', complained Don Guitierre Gomez Fuensalida, one of the many Spanish ambassadors sent to negotiate a marriage between Henry and Catherine, 'he is so subjugated that he does not speak a word except in response to what the king asks him'. According to Fuensalida the only way into the prince's bedroom was through his father's; Henry once became so angry with the lad that it seemed 'as if he sought to kill him', and he had to lock the boy up until his anger cooled. Fuensalida may have been prejudiced since Henry Tudor was trying to restrict access to the heir in order to prevent a Spanish marriage. Yet another witness, Reginald Pole, a cousin who knew the royal family fairly well, recalled that Henry Tudor disliked his son intensely, 'having no affection, or fancy unto him'.[12]

The effect of such treatment may be seen in Henry VIII's attitude to the pope – a father figure *par excellence*. As a young monarch Henry VIII published the *Defence of the Seven Sacraments* in 1520, an attack on Luther so vehement that it helped prompt Pope Leo X to award him the title of 'Defender of the Faith'. After the breakdown of his marriage to Catherine Henry turned to the pope. He did so in two seemingly contradictory ways: first as a penitent son to an understanding parent, and second as a politician owed a favour. 'Most blessed father,' Henry VIII wrote to Clement VII in February 1528, 'our fidelity and reverence towards your holiness and the Apostolic See is more firm and sure than ought to be expressed by messengers and the testimony of letters. Now, at this time, we, wholely confiding in your holiness's goodness and affection, fly to you as a suppliant.'[13] When the pope acted as a bad father (and faithless political debtor) by not merely refusing to grant a divorce, but suggesting that he take Anne Boleyn as his mistress, or even rid

20 *Henry VIII, Jane Seymour and Prince Edward*, after the style of Hans Holbein. This is an allegorical portrait, for Jane Seymour died after giving birth to Edward, shown here aged six or seven. It was intended to glorify Henry's family as an institution that provided him with an heir, and England with the stability that all believed could only be ensured by a king and an undisputed succession

21 *Prince Edward*, by Hans Holbein the Younger. Henry's desire for a male heir coincided with an increased interest in children and childhood. Painted when he was six, holding a pet monkey, this charming portrait shows the future Edward VI as something more than a little adult

himself of his wife in his own courts and forbid Catherine from appealing to Rome, Henry was as outraged as only those can be who see their expectations come to naught.[14]

Dependence and then rejection – such was the pattern of Henry's behaviour not just with the pope, but with many to whom he became attached. After serving the king faithfully for two decades, and carrying the vast burden of royal government upon his ample (and admittedly well-rewarded) shoulders, his chancellor Cardinal Wolsey was suddenly disgraced, and would surely have been executed had he not died of natural causes, brought on by old age and bitter disappointment, on his way to the Tower in 1530. Henry VIII's equally faithful though far more effective servant Thomas Cromwell was not so fortunate. After less than a decade's service, one of the most productive in English history, Henry precipitately ordered Cromwell's arrest whilst the latter was presiding over a meeting of the privy council, had him thrown into the Tower, and after a strenuous interrogation, he was beheaded for treason in July 1540. Seven years later the king turned upon his loyal and successful general the Duke of Norfolk, who would have followed his son, the Earl of Suffolk, to the scaffold on 28 January 1547, had not Henry died a few hours earlier, invalidating the royal signature on the death warrant. As Thomas More, Henry's friend, chancellor, and most famous victim remarked, the boon companion who walked for hours around More's garden in Chelsea with his arm about his shoulders, talking intimately about every subject under the sun, would have his head in a trice, if it 'could win him a castle in France'.[15]

This pattern of dependence and rejection was also apparent in Henry's relations with women. For instance, after their marriage he fell in love with Catherine of Aragon so quickly and deeply that less than three months later he wrote to his father-in-law that 'if we were still free we would still choose her for our wife before all other'.[16] Yet when she refused to divorce him (and by implication admit that she had been living in sin for two decades and her daughter was a bastard) Henry's anger knew no bounds. 'How contemptuously, uncharitably and disobediently,' he complained, 'she hath used and showed herself to us and our laws.'[17]

Henry was not a highly sexed man: he married six women not because he relished his libido, but because he could never come to terms with it. Ultimately the king made love more for procreation than for pleasure. The deaths of so many of his brothers and sisters had taught him the insecurity inherent in any royal succession, while the recent history of the Wars of the Roses reminded him, like all his subjects, of the dangers inherent in the absence of a generally accepted male heir. Thus the king was extremely grateful to Jane Seymour, his third wife, who died providing him with such an heir, Edward VI. Even though in life he may have loved her less than all his wives – except for Anne of Cleves, whom he never loved at all – he had himself buried beside her in St George's Chapel, Windsor.

Henry may well have had strong incestuous tendencies.[18] In middle age he easily convinced himself that he had sinned by marrying his brother's widow, and had thus incurred the Old Testament's punishment for those 'who hath uncovered his brother's nakedness: they shall be childless'.[19] He met Anne Boleyn through her elder sister, Mary, who had been his mistress for several years. After their marriage collapsed he accused Anne of incest with her brother George, and had both of them executed for this most heinous crime, of which they were completely innocent.

By trumping up this charge Henry may well have been indulging in the common psychological process known as 'projection' – accusing someone else of an offence of which one feels consciously or unconsciously guilty. For instance, in March 1527, in the midst of his own efforts to obtain a divorce, he wrote to his sister Margaret that the recent annulment of her marriage to the Earl of Angus (whom she had married in 1514) broke 'the divine ordinance of inseparable matrimony'. Whether Henry realized it or not, he echoed Catherine's objections to their divorce by reminding his sister that in ending her marriage she was not only ruining her reputation, but bastardizing her children. Henry was no better able to face up to the contradictions in his own actions than he was to those in his personality. Often he ignored them. Sometimes he appealed to his conscience, once telling the pope that it was dearer to him than Holy Mother Church. Frequently he would blame others, attributing, for example, his marital problems to his 'ill luck in meeting with such ill-conditioned wives'.

While to lose one wife might be attributed to bad luck, to lose four must be judged as more than downright carelessness. Quite simply, women both attracted and repelled the king. Having never had a close relationship with Elizabeth of York or some maternal substitute, Henry failed to reconcile that contradiction in the male psyche between the woman as a sexual object and the pure mother figure, which has been described as 'the whore/Madonna complex'. Henry's last two marriages revealed the ambivalence of his sexual

desires. He wanted a virginal yet experienced partner. Even though
Catherine Howard's relatives praised 'her pure and honest
condition', it is hard to believe that Henry (who had an acute ear
for court gossip) could have been unaware that she was notoriously
promiscuous. When Archbishop Cranmer eventually told the king
of Catherine's infidelities, he was shattered, and went into a severe
depression that lasted for a couple of years. His sixth wife, Catherine
Parr, helped him regain his spirits, for she was a woman of exemplary
virtue who, having been widowed, was also a partner of legitimate
experience.

Catherine's task was far from easy, for as the king grew older his
depressions returned and his health declined. He was pained by leg
ulcers, became a hypochondriac, and, as if he were trying to escape
from something he could not name, moved incessantly from place
to place. He grew more malevolent, toying with ministers, and even
his wife, with a sadism familiar to those who have witnessed a cat
playing with a mouse. In old age Henry cast aside the protections
he – like us all – had devised as a child to come to terms with the
adult, and often alien, world.[20] A little like someone who invents a
second personality in order to survive a troubled childhood, Henry
reverted to his real self. In the past he had deferred to others: to his
father, his grandmother, his tutors, even wives and ministers. Now
Henry wanted to be his own master, to let no ministers handle the
details, and thus determine the direction of policy. He embarked on
wars with France and Scotland that were as inept and mistaken as
they were ruinously expensive, for they forced the crown to squander
much of the monastic wealth confiscated in the Reformation, and to
debase the coinage, producing an inflation and a financial crisis that
lasted for well over a century. In sum, Henry in old age never
developed that 'ripeness' which Shakespeare maintained was the
reward of a life well lived: instead he showed a rottenness that arose
from one badly begun. With that ripe clarity which comes to those
who have lived a full life, as he lay dying in 1530 Cardinal Wolsey
summed up the contradictory nature of his master's personality: 'He
is a prince of royal courage and hath a princely heart, and rather
than he will miss or want part of his appetite he will hazard the loss
of one half of his kingdom.'[21]

V

ELIZABETH I

Elizabeth was born on 7 September 1533 in Greenwich Palace in a large ornate bed once given to England as tribute by the King of France, which her father had ordered taken out of storage for the occasion. Perhaps he hoped that in it would be brought forth the son he desperately wanted – the male heir, who might win glory fighting England's traditional enemy, and by simply being male would ensure the succession, and save the realm from the anarchy that seemed to blight all women's rule. The room in which Elizabeth was born proved to be more prophetic than the bed: it was known as the Chamber of the Virgins, from the tapestries of famous maids that adorned the walls. Equally auspicious was the date, 7 September, the Vigil of the Blessed Virgin Mary.

Yet few Catholics were to gain much pleasure from that coincidence, for Elizabeth was, quite literally, the child of the English Reformation. Her father had broken with Rome – among other reasons – in order to divorce Catherine of Aragon and marry Anne Boleyn, legitimizing the baby she was carrying. Thus Elizabeth could hardly become anything else than a Protestant. By the same token Mary, her elder half-sister – Catherine's child – had to remain a Catholic, who for the rest of her life blamed Elizabeth for her mother's disgrace, her own bastardy, and England's schisms. Elizabeth's parents also blamed her for not being born a boy: their reaction was, reported the Imperial ambassador, one of 'great disappointment and sorrow'.[1] Three years later Henry had her mother executed. So Elizabeth had not only to rule as a woman in a man's world, but to face a paternal rejection so strong that it remained with her until, at the end of a splendidly glorious reign, she turned her head to the wall, to die deeply depressed at her own sense of failure.

So in many ways the motifs that were to dominate the seven decades of Elizabeth's life had been set by the hour of her birth.

For the first three months of her life Elizabeth remained at Greenwich with her mother, before being taken to Hatfield, some twenty miles north of the capital. Initially Henry was very proud of his daughter. He ordered that she be shown off to the citizens of London, consulted the Archbishop of Canterbury about her weaning, and on hearing of Catherine of Aragon's death triumphantly carried her around the court. To Henry, Elizabeth was the precursor to the son whom he was sure Anne would bear. So when she failed to do so, miscarrying of her saviour by having a still-born boy in January 1536, the king's wrath was implacable. On 2 May Anne was arrested, and seventeen days later she was beheaded for treason, incest, and adultery.

After her mother's death Elizabeth's fortunes plummeted. In June 1536 parliament declared her illegitimate, incapable of inheriting the throne. In August her governess complained that the king's allowance would hardly keep her in food and clothing. 'She is as toward a child,' Lady Bryan went on, 'and as gentle of conditions, as I ever knew any in my life.'2 Elizabeth's contacts with her father and the court remained limited to formal occasions. In October 1537 he let her carry the robe at the christening of her younger brother, Edward.

As she grew up Elizabeth seemed to be searching for some mother figure. She had little contact with her father's third wife, Jane Seymour, a mousy girl whose only achievement, giving birth to a son, proved to be her undoing. Henry let her visit his fourth wife, the equine Anne of Cleves. She was grateful when the indiscreet Queen Catherine Howard invited her to dine in public.

Henry's last wife was to prove to have the most influence on her, becoming the closest person to a real mother the girl had ever known. At the time of his marriage to Catherine Parr in 1543 Elizabeth had for some unknown reason upset her father, who refused to see her. A year later in July 1544 she wrote to Catherine asking her to intercede with the king so he would forgive her, let her return to court, and so end 'my exile'.3 Catherine did so. Elizabeth's gratitude was boundless. She sent her stepmother Christmas presents of translations of devotional works, on which she had spent hours, writing them in her exquisite italic hand. The last few years of her father's reign were the happiest that Elizabeth had yet known. She and Edward became firm friends, sharing the same tutors, and enjoying the affection of a pious, good, and gentle woman, who brought them up in the new learning of humanism.

But – as Elizabeth was to learn time and time again – love never lasts forever. In January 1547 Edward Seymour, Duke of Somerset, told her and her brother of their father's death, that Edward was now king, and that he, as Lord Protector, would be regent during his nephew's minority. Four months later Elizabeth suffered another blow when her cherished stepmother betrayed her father's memory by secretly marrying Lord Admiral Thomas Seymour, the Lord Protector's younger brother. 'I cannot express to you', Elizabeth confided to Mary, 'how much affliction I suffered when I was informed of this marriage.'[4]

Elizabeth's sorrow soon changed to infatuation. A contemporary described her new stepfather as 'fierce in courage, courtly in fashion, in personage stately, in voice magnificent, but somewhat empty in matter'. An unscrupulous womanizer, he may even have tried to marry Elizabeth before hastily bedding Catherine, an old flame. At first Elizabeth lived with Catherine and Thomas in their houses at Hunsdon and Chelsea. Dressed only in his nightgown and slippers he started coming uninvited into Elizabeth's chamber early in the morning (having had keys made to all the rooms in the house). They would romp on her bed, the middle-aged man touching her back, tickling, smacking her bottom, pretending to get into bed with her. When Katherine Ashley, Elizabeth's faithful friend and servant, complained to Catherine she discounted it as nothing – mere puppy play. She even joined in. One day whilst walking in the garden she held the girl as her husband cut her dress to pieces with his sword. Soon Elizabeth recognized that Seymour was playing more than a game. On the threshold of womanhood she was both excited and frightened by him. Initially caution – maybe coquetry – prevailed. She started getting up early to be dressed and reading a book when Seymour came into her room. But soon afterwards she let him embrace her. When someone told Catherine, now four months pregnant, she was deeply hurt, and packed her stepdaughter off to stay with Sir Arthur Denny in Cheshunt.

From here Elizabeth sent her stepmother a guarded letter of apology. It was even more opaque than usual, since she could not admit in writing an offence that her nascent womanhood could but barely comprehend, particularly to the substitute mother who, she confessed, had shown her 'manifold kindnesses'.[5] Elizabeth fell ill, possibly from the complications of the menarche, suffering the onslaught of the migraines that were to torment her for over three more decades. She continued to reassure Seymour that 'I am a friend not won with trifles, nor lost with the like', and asked him for

The image bears the inscription: ANNA BOLINA VXOR · · · · HENRI· OCTA

22 *Anne Boleyn*, artist unknown. Elizabeth inherited her mother's looks and determination, but lacked her hysteria and gambler's instinct. She had little to do with Anne before Henry VIII executed her in 1536, and afterwards spoke of her mother but twice

news of her stepmother's health.⁶ So when Catherine Parr died in September from the complications of childbirth, her ambivalent feelings towards Seymour, and her sense of guilt at having betrayed her stepmother (which had already made her ill), must have exacerbated the guilt that always accompanies the death of those we love.

If Seymour felt such sentiments he overcame them with the manfulness of the inveterate Don Juan. Widowhood let him scheme for real where before he had merely gambolled in fun. He may even have sent Elizabeth a formal marriage proposal via her treasurer, Thomas Parry, with whom he was ostensibly negotiating about the lease of a house.

All this might not have amounted to much, and would have never been recorded for the sniggers of posterity, had Seymour's overweening ambitions not blanketed his stunted sense of discretion. Resenting his elder brother's power, he plotted to depose him, to seize the king, and marry Elizabeth without the privy council's approval. In January 1549 Lord Protector Somerset arrested Thomas Seymour for treason, as well as piracy and counterfeiting, and sent Sir Robert Tyrwhitt to Hatfield to interrogate Elizabeth. On being confronted with the charges she was 'marvellously abashed, and did weep tenderly a long time', which prompted Tyrwhitt to conclude his report to the council, 'I do see in her face that she is guilty.'⁷ By the second interrogation she had regained her composure. While confessing to the early morning romp – which were more slips of silliness than acts of treason – and admitting that she and Kat Ashley had giggingly discussed Seymour as a possible husband, she maintained that they had always agreed that she would never marry him, or anyone else, without the government's permission. Equally firmly she denied the rumours 'that I am in the Tower, and with child by my Lord Admiral'. To disprove such 'shameful slanders', she wrote to Somerset that 'I shall most heartily desire your Lordship that I may come to the Court after your first determination; that I may show myself there as I am'.⁸ Fortunately Elizabeth did not have to appear before the privy council to prove herself still a maid, for Kat Ashley's and Thomas Parry's confessions, extorted in the Tower, agreed with her own. 'They all sing one song,' Tyrwhitt lamented.⁹ Then Elizabeth counter-attacked, demanding that the government issue a proclamation that the rumours about her were 'but lies', and that they free her servants from prison as a token of her innocence.

Elizabeth also recognized that the whole incident had tarnished her reputation. After Ashley's and Parry's release, she cultivated Mrs

Tyrwhitt, a dry, pious lady, whom the privy council appointed her governess. She wrote affectionate letters to her brother, Edward VI, saying how much she enjoyed his 'delightful society', having from 'your tender infancy . . . ever been your fondest sister'.

Within a couple of years it was becoming plain to all that the poor boy was dying of tuberculosis, and that Mary would become queen and England Catholic once again. To prevent this calamity, and to maintain his own influence as regent (from which office he had ousted Somerset in 1550), the Duke of Northumberland plotted to replace Mary with his daughter-in-law, Lady Jane Grey, Henry VIII's great-niece. But on Edward's death in July 1553, Elizabeth refused to cooperate, rejecting Northumberland's offer of land and money if she would give up her claim to the throne, and come to London to support the new regime. Instead she said she was too ill to move, sending a doctor's certificate to prove it. He must have been a skilled medical man, for five days later, after the failure of Northumberland's coup, Elizabeth was well enough to ride in triumph into London with her sister, as the crowds cheered their new queen, and by implication the principle of legitimate succession which was Elizabeth's only hope for the future.

The two sisters were an ill-matched pair: one a Papist spinster of thirty-eight, the other a striking Protestant maid of twenty. Not surprisingly they soon quarrelled. Mary had always blamed Elizabeth for her mother's divorce and her own bastardy. Elizabeth could not swallow her sister's faith – quite literally so. Even though she asked Mary for copes, chasubles, and chalices so she could celebrate the mass, and after much pressure attended one, she loudly complained that 'all this way her stomach ached'. Mary rightly concluded that her sister 'only went to mass out of hypocrisy'. Both were relieved when Elizabeth left court in December 1553.

Far more important that the condition of Elizabeth's soul – or even the state of her digestion – was her role as a Protestant alternative to a Papist queen who was becoming increasingly unpopular. Mary's decision, taken against the council's advice, to marry Philip of Spain prompted a number of gentlemen led by Sir Thomas Wyatt to plot to depose Mary and replace her with Elizabeth, whom they would marry to Edward Courtenay, Earl of Devon, and Edward IV's great-grandson. When this feckless youth talked indiscreetly, he alerted the authorities, forcing Wyatt to rise prematurely, and so not only ensured the rebellion's failure but placed Elizabeth in mortal peril.

Learning of the conspiracy on 26 January 1554 Mary ordered her

KATHARINE PARRE

23 *Catherine Parr*, artist unknown. Henry VIII's sixth, and last, wife was almost like a real mother to Elizabeth. She educated the young princess widely and well, but on Henry VIII's death betrayed her by marrying the unscrupulous Thomas Seymour

24 *Thomas, Lord Seymour of Sudeley,* artist unknown. To this adventurer whose machinations ended in his own execution, the fourteen-year-old Elizabeth lost her heart – and nearly her head

sister to court, where she would in effect be a prisoner. Elizabeth
tried the excuse she had so effectively employed with Northumberland, claiming to be too ill to leave her country house at Ashridge,
in Buckinghamshire, for London. Mary sent her own doctors to
examine the princess. They reported that even though her feet were
badly swollen, and her kidneys inflamed (possibly from scarlet
fever), she could survive the thirty-five-mile journey if it were taken
in easy stages.

So on 12 February 1554, the day that her friend Lady Jane Grey
was beheaded, Elizabeth was carried out of Ashridge on a litter. She
could only bear a few miles a day, and by the time she reached
Highgate the swelling in her knees was so bad that she could hardly
move the joints. She had to rest for nearly a week before she could
endure the ride down the hill into the city. As she was carried from
the City to Westminster on 22 February she drew back the curtains
of her litter so the people could see her, dressed in white, looking
deathly pale, and, the Imperial ambassador complained, 'proud and
haughty'. The sick young woman saw a sight that made her even
more frightened – the butchered remains of those executed for taking
part in the Wyatt conspiracy swinging from gibbets, their heads on
pikes adorning the city gates. On her arrival at Whitehall Palace
Mary refused to see Elizabeth, ordering her held incommunicado
for three weeks whilst the privy council argued over her fate. The
Lord Chancellor Stephen Gardiner urged that 'so long as Elizabeth
lived he had no hope of seeing the kingdom at peace'. Other councillors were, however, more cautious. Elizabeth was still Henry VIII's
daughter, and the only undisputed heir in case Mary died childless.
On 15 March the council decided that Elizabeth had better go to the
Tower. The next day the Marquis of Winchester and the Earl of
Sussex arrived to escort her there. Petrified, she demanded to be
allowed to write to her sister. After some hesitation Winchester and
Sussex agreed.

'I pray to God I may die the shamefullest death that any ever
died,' Elizabeth told Mary, if ever she had 'practised, counselled nor
consented to anything that might be prejudicial to your person
anyway or dangerous to the state by any means.' She begged that she
might be allowed to see the queen, and not, like Thomas Seymour, be
condemned to the Tower unheard. After writing just over a page
Elizabeth ended her terrified, and often garbled, denial of any
involvement with 'the traitor Wyatt', by crossing through the blank
remainder of the paper to prevent the government from using the

space to insert a forged confession.[10] Mary refused to read the letter, exclaiming that her father would have never tolerated such impertinence. All the 'tide letter' did was ensure that Elizabeth's barge missed the tide for shooting London Bridge, delaying her entry into the Tower for less than a day.

When her barge arrived at Traitors' Gate on the morning of Palm Sunday, 17 March, John Foxe, author of the immensely popular contemporary history *Actes and Monuments of these latter and perilous dayes* (1563) recorded that Elizabeth refused to enter.[11] Sitting on the ground in the rain she declared, 'Here landeth as true subject, being prisoner, as ever landeth at these stairs, and before thee, O God! I speak it, having no friends but thee alone.' To the Yeomen of the Guard waiting to march her to the Bell Tower, she said, 'I never thought to come here as a prisoner, and I pray you all, good friends and fellows, bear me witness that I come in no traitor, but as true a woman to the Queen's majesty as any is now living: and thereupon will take my death.' Only the tears of a gentleman usher, and the reassurance of the Lieutenant of the Tower, persuaded the princess to enter the prison where she was convinced she would – like her mother – meet her death.

She nearly did. When Lord Chancellor Gardiner, and nine other councillors, came to cross-examine her, they asked why Wyatt had written advising her to go to Donnington Castle in Berkshire, and thus move further from the government in London. Panic-stricken she said she had never heard of the place. Then, pulling herself together, she admitted that Donnington was one of her estates, but denied ever having received Wyatt's letter. 'Might I not, My Lords,' she insisted, 'go to mine own house?' Her answer, and the government's failure to show that she had actually seen Wyatt's letter, won over the Earl of Arundel. Perhaps he accepted her story because, as he told her, 'Your Grace saith true,' or else because he wanted to keep Elizabeth in reserve in case Mary did not implement the pro-Spanish foreign policy that he favoured.

Mary's torturers failed to extract any information that might incriminate her sister. Although 'tossed marvellously' upon the rack, Sir James Croft, Wyatt's accomplice, refused to implicate Elizabeth, even though he had visited her at Ashridge just before the uprising. In the speech he gave before being hanged, drawn and quartered – the punishment for treason that could be excruciatingly prolonged for the uncooperative – Wyatt insisted that Elizabeth had played no part in the plot.

25 *Princess Elizabeth*, aged about thirteen, artist unknown. There is something terribly vulnerable about this precocious, grave child on the threshold of womanhood. She holds a book, and another stands open on the table beside her, symbols of her considerable learning

ANNO DNI · 1 5 4 4 ·

LADI MAR[ ] DOVGHTER TO
T[ ] MOST · VERTVOVS · PRINCE ·
KING · HENRI THE · EIGHT

THE · AGE · OF · XXVIII · YERES

26 *Princess Mary*, 1544, by Master John. In 1554 Mary sent her sister to the Tower, under suspicion of involvement in the Wyatt conspiracy. This portrait, one of the few painted of Mary as a princess, catches the fierce emotional and religious determination that made her reign a failure, and such a perilous time for her younger sister

So on 19 May the government had to release her from the Tower into the custody of Sir Henry Bedingfield, a stolid Norfolk squire, who was to take her to Woodstock, some ten miles north of Oxford. She passed her first night in his charge at Richmond, where she was convinced, Foxe tells us, that she would be murdered in her bed. She was much relieved to wake up to find that the rest of her journey was a public triumph: at High Wycombe housewives pressed home-baked cakes into her hands; at Aston the villagers rang the bells; at Rycote Lord Williams so 'marvellously well entertained her', that the queen sent him a reprimand.[12]

Woodstock was an anticlimax. Only four of the rooms in the decaying manor house were habitable, so Sir Thomas Parry had to lodge in the adjacent Bull Inn. Although Elizabeth baited her jailer, perhaps to keep up her spirits, Bedingfield treated her correctly. When he told her she could not write to Mary, she complained that she was treated worse than the meanest prisoners in Newgate, for they were at least allowed to petition their sovereign. When she fell ill with inflamed kidneys and Bedingfield forbad her to consult her own doctors, suggesting instead that she call in two local physicians from Oxford, she refused 'to make any strangers privy to the state of my body, but commit it to God'.[13] When she asked him for an English Protestant Bible, Bedingfield demurred, offering her Ovid and the Psalms instead. On hearing a milkmaid sing in the park outside Elizabeth broke down, lamenting that the girl's lot was far happier than her own.

But Elizabeth had at least survived, and (if Foxe's story is correct) she admitted as much in the doggerel she scratched on a window with a diamond:

> *Much suspected by me,*
> *Nothing proved can be,*
> *quoth Elizabeth, prisoner.*[14]

After ten miserable months at Woodstock Mary ordered Elizabeth's release. For the rest of her reign the two sisters remained distant. The elder became more bitter after she failed to conceive a child, the Spanish husband with whom she had fallen passionately and pathetically in love returned home, and the burning of heretics seemed only to inspire Protestantism. The younger bided her time, surviving other threats because Philip intervened so he might marry her off to some ally, and because she had learned enough discretion to avoid being entrapped by the Dudley conspiracy of 1556. A year later on 17 November Mary died, and, as Foxe wrote, 'after so long restrainment, so great dangers escaped, such blusterous storms overblown, so many injuries digested, and wrongs sustained', Elizabeth inherited her father's throne.[15]

The problems facing the twenty-five-year-old queen were immense. 'I never saw', Sir Thomas Smith recalled, 'England weaker in strength, men, money and riches.'[16] Armagil Waad was even more pessimistic: 'The Queen poor, the realm exhausted, the nobility poor and decayed. Want of good captains, and soldiers. The people out of order. Justice not executed. All things dear.'[17]

Foxe's history (which Elizabeth may even have helped write) facilitated the resolution of this crisis by providing queen and people with the legend of the Protestant heroine overcoming immense trials to win her just reward. Foxe is not a completely reliable source. There is, for example, no basis for his story that Gardiner sent a death warrant to the Tower that lacked Queen Mary's signature in the hope that it would be enough to persuade the Lieutenant to execute Elizabeth. But Foxe's version of the past immediately became the orthodoxy that glorified the queen; it enhanced her self-esteem and her reputation, placing the Elizabethan Settlement in a logical historical context.

Elizabeth's education also helped her make this settlement in several ways. Her tutors, Roger Ascham, Anthony Coke, John Cheke, Richard Cox, and William Grindal, had nurtured her considerable talents and curiosity, educating her in the humanistic learning of the Reformation. In doing so they provided the intellectual foundations for the religious settlement which was, in a sense, her birthright. All Cambridge men, these teachers connected her with a group of Cambridge-educated advisers, such as Sir William Cecil and Sir Nicholas Bacon, who helped shape her regime. Apart from the obvious advantages their education gave her – such as being able to speak to ambassadors in their own languages – it enabled Elizabeth to overcome male prejudices. 'Her mind is exempt from female weakness, and she is endowed with a masculine power of application,' rhapsodized her most influential teacher, Roger Ascham.[18] Her educational achievements also gave Elizabeth considerable self-confidence. As a young woman she sent her brother a portrait of herself, enclosing a note: 'For the face, I grant, I might well blush to offer, but the mind I shall never be ashamed to present.' A generation later she boasted to parliament that 'few that be no Professors had read more' than she had.[19]

Queen Elizabeth needed all the confidence she could get, for her father had severely damaged her ego, while paradoxically making her more resolute and sure of herself. Although Elizabeth hardly ever mentioned her mother, except in connection with her execution, she constantly evoked Henry VIII's memory. 'She prides herself in him,' the Venetian ambassador reported in 1557; 'everyone says she resembles him.'[20] She both admired her father and was not a little awed, even resentful, of him. Sometimes she let the ambivalence show, once claiming 'as good a courage . . . as ever my father had'. Throughout her life she had to reconcile her esteem for the magnificent Henry VIII, with her fear of the cruel man who, when she was nearly three, a highly impressionable age, turned from being a proud papa into the ogre who killed her mother and rejected her. Perhaps she did so in a letter she wrote to her dying brother:

> I consider that, as a good father that loves his child dearly, doth punish him sharply, so God, favouring your Majesty greatly, hath chastised you straightly. And as a father doth it for the good of the child, so God prepared this for the better health of your grace.[21]

There can be no doubt that Henry's disappointment that she was a girl not only made Elizabeth try and prove herself – sometimes more as a king than a queen – but hampered her development as a woman.

The one thing everyone knows about Elizabeth is that she was the Virgin Queen. Yet whether she chose this state because of some Machiavellian machination or a Freudian frigidity no one can say for sure.

Elizabeth had sound political reasons for not marrying. As a single woman she could trail her coat across England and Europe. Every eligible bachelor – and many ineligible ones – pursued the proferred carrot. Even so hopeless a donkey as Philip II thought that he had a chance. Elizabeth kept his daydreams going so astutely that he delayed sending the Armada for a decade during which the English navy waxed as the Spanish waned. If she married she would – as all men believed she should – become subservient to her husband. If she chose a foreigner (like Philip) he would make England a puppet to an alien power. If she selected an Englishman she would render the throne prey to her husband's ambitions, and those of his family and friends.

Although the political advantages of remaining single were obvious to posterity, the dangers of doing so terrified contemporaries. Time and time again parliament begged the queen to marry and have an heir. If she died without issue – as she nearly did from smallpox in 1562, and chickenpox in 1572 – the results would have been catastrophic. Today Elizabeth would be castigated as the foolish virgin whose frigid selfishness condemned England to a civil war that the hatreds of the Reformation would have made even more destructive than the Wars of the Roses.

Without question Elizabeth liked men. She welcomed their advances. She relished their compliments, if not their caresses. When she heard of the death of the Duke of Alençon, her last suitor, she wept bitterly. She may even have lost her heart to Robert Dudley, Earl of Leicester, and might well have married him had his wife not died in suspicious circumstances. Did she refuse to do so because her political sensitivities told her that such promiscuity (like Mary Queen of Scots' affairs) would shock her subjects to the very limits of loyalty? Leicester did not think so. Six years later he confided, 'I believe not in truth that the Queen will ever marry. I have known her from her eighth year better than any man upon earth. From that date she declared she would never marry.'[22]

Elizabeth's virginity, her inability to consummate a relationship, to give wholly of her mind and body, may well have come from two sources. First her sense of self-esteem as a woman, her opinion of her sex being very weak. She constantly apologized for being female as if to assuage her father's disappointment, claiming 'Princely virtue beyond her sex'. Complaining to James VI about the behaviour of the Scots ambassador she wrote, 'though I were of the female sex I could never endure such affronts'.[23] When in her speech to the troops assembled at Tilbury to repulse the Armada she said, 'I know I have the body of but a weak and feeble woman, but I have the heart and stomach of a king, and a King of England,' was she alluding to Henry VIII, the last monarch to lead Englishmen into battle?

Elizabeth's decision not to marry also came from a more complex and deep-rooted feeling. Since the threshold of consciousness she had learned that death was the price of giving oneself to a man. Her father had chopped off her mother's head when Elizabeth was nearly three, and executed Catherine Howard, who had befriended her, when she was eight. Two years later Catherine Parr nearly followed the others to the block. Catherine remarried for love, only to die giving birth to the child of the adventurer who betrayed her with the stepdaughter she had nurtured like a real mother. At fourteen

27 *Robert Dudley, Earl of Leicester*, after the Flemish School. If Elizabeth had ever been able to overcome her adolescent traumas and marry, she would probably have chosen Robert Dudley. But a combination of political caution and emotional frigidity prevented her from giving herself to the man who knew her, perhaps, better than any other

28 *Elizabeth I*, about 1575, artist unknown. This official portrait, executed when the queen was in the full glory of her majesty, already shows signs of the formalized style that was part of a deliberate attempt to turn an aging woman into the eternal Gloriana

Elizabeth nearly gave herself to the same unscrupulous Lothario, who toyed with her affections and jeopardized her life before perishing on the scaffold. On hearing of Seymour's execution the princess was reputed to have said, 'This day died a man of much wit, but little judgment.'

Emotion, far more than political sagacity, prompted Elizabeth not only to remain a virgin, but to turn her unfulfilled love for one man into an affair with the whole of her people. At her coronation she dressed as a bride riding to marry the nation. When two years later a parliamentary delegation begged her to wed and have children, she took off her wedding ring saying, 'I am already bound unto a husband, which is the kingdom of England.' And she kept her word. Although as she grew older she changed from being the young bride to what her godson, John Harington, called 'this state's regal mother', she wore the ring until it had to be prised from her dead finger.[24]

The queen wooed her subjects through a series of pageants, processions, and displays. She walked among crowds working them with a combination of lady-like modesty and the politician's charisma. She enthralled – and controlled – her courtiers with the artifice of courtly love, turning the sensual into the platonic. Old men such as Burghley could pledge fealty to a daughter figure. Young blades such as Sir Walter Ralegh, Sir Christopher Hatton, or the Earl of Essex could buzz about the queen bee, sometimes like gallants, and at others like petulant sons, sure – unless they were as headstrong as Essex – that they could sip the honey without getting stung.

Elizabeth, however, had to suffer many scars before enjoying the sweetness of her patrimony. A week before Mary died the Imperial ambassador described a long interview he had just had with the princess. 'She is highly indignant at the things that have been done against her during her sister's reign. She is much attached to the people, and is very confident that they are on her side (which is indeed true).'[25] Elizabeth lived long enough to become queen because she instinctively realized (as she showed in the Seymour affair, and the Wyatt conspiracy), that ultimately she had to depend on public opinion. Thus, after reigning for thirty-nine years, she could truthfully boast to parliament, 'There will never Queen sit in my seat with more zeal to my country, care for my subjects . . . than myself.'[26]

From her earliest years Elizabeth hid her true feelings. For instance, on hearing at the age of thirteen that her stepmother had secretly married less than four months after her father's death, she wrote to Mary, 'Neither you, nor I, dearest sister, are in any condition as to offer any obstacle thereunto without running risk of making our own lot much worse than it is . . . I think then that the best course we can take is that of discretion.'[27] A few months later she ignored her own advice to become ensnared with Seymour. The episode reinforced her caution, saving her from being implicated in the Wyatt conspiracy. Her willingness to go along, superficially at least, with the re-established Catholic church was later reflected in her policy as queen not to have windows cut into any man's soul: all she required was a decent, open conformity. 'Stay or qualify your passions,' she advised Mary Queen of Scots, 'it is not the manner to obtain good things with evil speeches, nor benefits with injurious challenges.'[28] Elizabeth delayed executing Mary for over a decade not just because her own experiences helped her empathize with the predicament of someone around whom conspiracies swirled, or because she feared the political consequences, but because her own survival had in large part been due to avoiding action for as long as possible. Twice, for instance, she had pleaded ill health in the hope of staying on the sidelines and letting time take its course.

And when it did, and she came to the throne, she recognized her debt to time. In 1558 during her coronation procession through London, she stopped to address an allegorical figure of Time, one of the many tributes that lined the streets. 'Time hath brought me hither,' acknowledged the queen.[29] But unlike many monarchs, who come to the throne because of an accident of birth and from no skill of their own, Elizabeth had also (to use her own phrase), 'been miraculously preserved at sundry times'.[30] As queen she used the skills that had enabled her to survive her childhood and youth to give her nation time: time to discover new worlds, both at home and abroad, without the religious turmoil that plagued the Continent; time to let parliament develop, the economy grow, for her people to realize their genius, be it at sea, on the stage, or in the simple routine of a family life well lived. A childhood which she admitted had been fraught with 'good experience and trial of this world', made possible the glories of an epoch that is quite rightly called Elizabethan.[31]

VI

CHARLES I

On 1 February 1624, Bishop William Laud stood behind Prince Charles at dinner. Charles was, Laud noted in his diary, exceedingly merry, talking about a wide range of subjects, including the choice of a career. One thing, declared the twenty-three-year-old prince, he could never be was a lawyer, because 'I cannot defend a bad nor yield in a good cause'.[1] Twenty-five years and two days later Charles walked out on to the black-draped scaffold in Whitehall to be executed defending the best cause he ever knew.

It would, of course, be absurd to suggest that just because Prince Charles told Laud he could never compromise, King Charles inevitably had to suffer martydom – the ultimate act of resistance. Many events came between Charles's youthful declaration and his dignified death. He was unlucky in war, social changes made England harder to govern, a financial crisis weakened his government, Scotland and Ireland rebelled against English hegemony, Puritans and Arminians seized much of the middle ground vital for religious tranquillity, parliament became more aggressive, and the king's enemies more intransigent. None the less in bringing about his death Charles played the crucial role. The decisions to depend on the notorious Duke of Buckingham, to dissolve his first four parliaments, to force the Scots to accept a new prayer book, to declare war on parliament in 1642, and the failure to find an effective peace afterwards, were all essentially the king's. They came from a personality that had been shaped by the time of that youthful declaration never to yield in a good cause, nor defend a bad one. Indeed, a year earlier, after a long interview with the heir to the throne, the Venetian ambassador wrote home, 'The coldness of his nature even in actions becoming his youth is not, perhaps, a good sign'. Charles's personality, the ambassador concluded, may 'have been repressed, possibly by an unfortunate education'.[2]

Charles was born on 19 December 1600, the third child and second son of King James VI of Scotland. Wet nurses and nannies looked after him in his nursery, which Lady Margaret Ochiltree supervised with a generous grant from the king. On the death of Elizabeth I in March 1603 James became King of England, and straight away rushed south to enjoy what he called 'the promised land'. A few weeks later he was followed by the rest of the royal family, except for Charles, who was too frail to make the arduous journey. He remained in Scotland for over a year until his parents thought he was strong enough to travel in slow leisurely stages to join them. Soon after he was reunited with the king and queen, they committed him to the guardianship of Lady Elizabeth Carey. She seems to have treated the boy with affection, protecting him from his father's more outrageous suggestions on his upbringing, such as the wearing of iron braces on his legs to help him walk, and with good food she cured Charles of the rickets that had plagued him since infancy.[3]

While we do not know as much about the quality and detail of Charles's earliest years as, for example, those of his contemporary Louis XIII of France, three aspects of his childhood seem significant. First – like all royal children – he was brought up outside his own family, and in later life never displayed much concern or affection for his nurses and nannies which might indicate memories of a happy or satisfying childhood. Second, at the crucially important age of three his mother and father deserted him for a year, and after a brief reunion put him out again into the care of strangers. Third, throughout his earliest years he was an extremely weak child, who had serious problems learning to talk and walk. He may have expressed his frustration in the violent tantrums which contemporaries noted. Or else (as one of his first biographers suggested) he overcame his physical weaknesses by strenuous exercise, such as riding, hunting, and jogging, which in later life made him determined to the point of pig-headedness.[4] Certainly being separated from his parents, farmed out to people of whom he never became particularly fond, and a general sense of physical malaise did little to help Charles come to terms with his own family.

Most children's consciousness of their family dates back to their earliest memories: mother, father, elder brothers and sisters are something that have always been there. But for a child raised outside the family they are distant figures who come and go, making demands on his affections that may conflict with those felt for nannies, and which increase as the child grows older and (as was the custom) spends more time at court with his real family.

Charles's mother, Anne of Denmark, was a remote figure. Unhappy in her marriage, piously Catholic in her faith, she had little influence at court. Her subsequent claim that Charles was her favourite child is credible only because her relations with her other two surviving children were so bad. His sister, Elizabeth, was an upright though equally distant being: no childhood letters between the two have survived. To his youngest son James was as generous with his purse as he was mean with his time. He was too inflexible – and too involved with his pretty young men – to have much positive influence on the boy. Threatened by his heir, the widely respected Prince Henry, the ageing king exacerbated relations between his two sons. Once, James threatened to leave the crown to Charles if Henry did not pursue his studies with more diligence. In retaliation Henry teased Charles mercilessly. One day, as the two were waiting with a group of bishops and courtiers for the king to appear, Henry snatched the Archbishop of Canterbury's hat and put it on Charles's head, saying that when he became king he would make him primate: he was enough of a swot and a toady for the job, and anyway the long clerical robes would hide his ugly ricket-ridden legs. Charles had to be dragged off screaming with anger. Henry showed his brother little affection: he treated appointments to Charles's household, and hence the choice of his friends and guardians, as a source of political patronage, taking scant notice of the boy's feelings. So, like many a threatened weakling, Charles tried to buy off the bully. 'Sweet, Sweet brother,' he wrote to Henry when he was nine, 'I will give everything I have to you, both horses, and my books, and my pieces [guns], and my crossbow, or anything you would have. Good brother love me . . .'[5]

Charles's efforts to win – or buy – his brother's love, and find someone to protect him, all came to naught in late 1611. After playing a strenuous game of tennis, Henry came down with typhoid fever from which he died on 6 November at the age of eighteen. His last request was for Elizabeth.

Henry's unexpected death was one of two traumas that affected Charles within less than half a year. Few princes have been as widely or deeply mourned as Henry. 'Our rising sun is set,' eulogized the Earl of Dorset, ' 'ere scarcely he did shine.' Unmindful of the younger brother, the poet John Donne wondered who could possibly fill the void. Charles may even have agreed. Immediately after Henry's death he fell ill, surely from psychosomatic causes. The public outpouring of grief, and the rapidly unfulfilled expectations

29 *Charles, Duke of York*, aged about four, by Robert Peake. Charles was a sickly child whose early portraits have a haunted yet awkward look. Even though Peake tried to hide the boy's infirmities, the effects of rickets clearly show through the richly embroidered robe. The boy stands badly, unsure where to put his hands or feet that the new heir would become 'the illustrious hope of Great Britain', did nothing to alleviate Charles's loss, or enhance his slight and much-battered self-confidence.[6] For years, it seemed as if Henry's ghost haunted him. In 1616, for instance, at his investiture as Prince of Wales the Bishop of Ely made the slip – surely a Freudian one – of praying for Prince Henry and not Prince Charles.[7] Two years later Charles latched on to his father's favourite, George Villiers, Duke of Buckingham, as a surrogate elder brother. In 1639, as his attempt to rule without parliament was about to come crashing down in failure, Charles christened his third son Henry, perhaps to evoke the memory of his immensely popular and promising brother.

The second trauma that Charles experienced in late childhood was a bitter-sweet one. In October 1611 Frederick, the Elector Palatine, ruler of lands in central and western Germany, came to England to court Princess Elizabeth. Charles formally greeted him as he landed at Westminster Steps. The two quickly became friends, perhaps because the German reminded Charles of the brother he had just lost. Anyway, Frederick and Elizabeth fell in love with an intensity marvellously rare for a diplomatic alliance. They were married, appropriately enough, on St Valentine's Day 1612. Charles spent much time with the young couple, enjoying an intimacy with his sister that he had never before known. When Frederick set off for Dover to take his young bride back to Germany, Charles rode with them as far as he could, lingering in Canterbury for a week, before James ordered him back to his usual bland routine. This brief friendship profoundly affected Charles. Following the outbreak of the Thirty Years War (1618–48), and the expulsion by Catholic troops of Frederick and Elizabeth from the Palatinate, Charles became one of their most ardent partisans. At the age of nineteen he found a cause (a common enough discovery for any adolescent), vowing – if his father gave permission – to lead a crusade across Europe to rescue the Lady Elizabeth and slay the Papist dragon. After he became king in 1625 the restoration of the Palatinate was the chief goal of Britain's foreign policy for over two decades. On Frederick's death in 1632 Charles virtually adopted his sister's children, assuring them, 'I will now occupy the place of the deceased.'[8] And for most of the Civil War, Prince Maurice and Prince Rupert did more than enough to repay that debt by fighting wholeheartedly for their uncle's cause.

During the traumatic winter of 1611 and spring of 1612 Charles's household arrangements were painfully disturbed. Just before Henry's death James removed Charles from Lady Carey's care to that of four male governors. Although the change from the custody of a governess to governors was usual for princes of Charles's age, it deprived him during a particularly difficult time of the help of the woman who had looked after him for the past eight years. Immediately after Henry's death James ordered that Charles should live in the royal household, where he could keep an eye on his heir. However, the king soon realized that his second son (unlike his first) was more of a bother than a threat, and sent him back to his own reconstituted household.

Here Charles remained for a half decade that was noteworthy mainly for its lack of incident. In 1613 he was confirmed; in 1614 he rode with James to open the Addled Parliament; in 1615 he visited Cambridge University; in 1616 he stood in for the king at the Garter service and was made Prince of Wales – all in all not much activity for the heir to the three kingdoms and a principality. One explanation for this withdrawal from public life is that it was a period of extended melancholia. Charles had just lost a brother to death and a sister in marriage. Overcoming such a bereavement is a painful process, a job at which the mind must work until it has come to accept the new reality. By and large people's ability to complete this depends on the strength of their self-identity. Charles was poorly prepared to carry out the job. He suffered his loss at the age of twelve, too young for a sufficiently resilient self-identity to have developed, particularly after a bruising childhood.

Charles's mother was of little help in dealing with this crisis. Having farmed her son out to other women, she had enjoyed little intimacy with him. She refused to attend Henry's funeral, forcing Charles to walk in the cortège as chief mourner in her stead. She opposed her daughter's marriage with a coldness that contrasted with the warmth Charles felt. His actions at the queen's death in 1619 betray his feelings towards her. When he heard that his mother was dangerously ill he rushed to Hampton Court, sleeping in the chamber next to hers. Thus he solicitously managed to persuade his mother to leave him, and not her faithful Danish maid, Anna, all her personal estate.[9] At his mother's funeral one observer noted that Charles mourned 'with a just measure of grief, without any affected sorrow'.[10] Afterwards he did not withdraw into himself, as was his usual reaction to an intensely felt loss. Altogether Anne's effect on her son was basically negative: by failing to establish a warm and close relationship with him – or providing the proverbial English nanny as a substitute – she made it hard for him to form relationships

30 *Anne of Denmark*, by Paul Van Somer. As a child and adolescent Charles had little to do with his mother, being brought up by a governess, Lady Elizabeth Carey. James's homosexuality had destroyed his marriage to Anne long before Charles, their youngest surviving child, was born. Here depicted out hunting, surrounded by her dogs, with Oatlands Palace in the background, the queen shows she had interests other than her family

31 *Henry, Prince of Wales*, about 1610, by Robert Peake. A strikingly handsome, promising and popular heir to the throne, Henry died suddenly at the age of eighteen. Although bullied by his elder brother, Charles was so profoundly affected by his death that during adolescence he retreated into his own world. He emerged only to become dependent on a substitute sibling, the Duke of Buckingham with other people, particularly women, and deprived him of 'that confidence of success that often induces real success', which Freud called 'the legacy of a mother's favour'.

Charles's father was equally useless in bolstering the boy's self-confidence. In his letters to the king Charles tried to win James's attention, if not his love. But the king rejected the overtures of 'His Majesty's most humble and obedient son and servant' to 'so good a father'. He refused, for instance, to let Charles accompany him on the royal visit to Scotland in 1617, notwithstanding the lad's pathetic pleas that he might be allowed to go and see the land of his birth. The boy seemed to embarrass James. When during a visit to the University of Cambridge in 1615 a don described the heir as 'Jacobissime Carole' and 'Jacobale', the king appeared angry at these references to 'a very James-like Charles' and 'a little James'.[11]

James much preferred the role of schoolmaster, where he could keep his distance, and thus hide his flaws, to the more intimate and vulnerable one of father. He spent little time with his children, instead writing textbooks, such as *Basilikon Doron*, for their edification. 'The state of monarchy is the supremest thing on earth', taught the king in a classic definition of the divine right of monarchy. 'For kings are not only God's lieutenants on earth, and sit upon God's throne, but even by God himself they are called Gods.' Such precepts, reinforced by numerous sermons, his tutors, and the study of his father's writings, helped shape Charles's superego. Although he would not, of course, have understood that modern term, he was familiar with his conscience. And Charles's conscience was a mighty force! His letters and personal papers show it was one of the most important influences in his life – if not the dominant one. 'I thank God', he wrote to his son, '[that my conscience] is dearer to me than a thousand kingdoms.'[12] The inflexibility of his conscience helps explain why the king first declared war on his subjects in 1642, and after his defeat four years later refused at the conference table to yield to his opponents the concessions they believed God had awarded them on the field of battle. Charles's conscience was not, however, inviolate: it was malleable enough to let him cede too little too late, and then permit him to renege on promises extracted under duress. When Charles went against his conscience, as he did with the signing of the Earl of Strafford's death warrant in 1641, his mental anguish was excruciating. For the rest of his life he was convinced that the Civil War was God's punishment for this betrayal.

When Charles followed the dictates of his conscience the result was very different. As a poem attributed to his last days affirmed:[13]

> *Close thine eyes and sleep secure,*
> *Thy soul is safe, thy body sure . . .*
> *A quiet conscience on thy breast*
> *Has only peace, has only rest.*

From his father's teachings Charles also developed strongly held convictions about the divine right of kings. To modern ears the claim to be almost a god seems arrant nonsense, but during the sixteenth and seventeenth centuries it was one that the most sensible of monarchs accepted. Queen Elizabeth advanced it. Yet she was prepared to give the Almighty a helping hand by manipulating the political system, even by using bribery, so His anointed might get her way. In contrast Charles assumed that since God had consecrated him as sovereign, all his subjects would obey him without question – or patronage and bribes. So the doctrine of monarchy by divine right saved an essentially lazy man from the daily grind of detailed government. It provided an uncertain man with the salve of godly certainty. It prompted him into those acts of intemperate resolution that are the hallmark of the truly irresolute. In sum, as far as Charles was concerned, the divine right of kings was a theological manna that satisfied a pyschological hunger.

The doctrines of divine right further complicated Charles's coming of age. Like the Oedipus of Greek legend, Charles was an heir for whom the fulfilment of his adult role of becoming king implied, consciously or not, wishing his father dead. To the sin of patricide might be added the equally heinous crime of regicide, for by rebelling against his father as *pater familias* – as all sons must – he was also attacking the king as *pater patriae* – something only traitors do. This implied trying to destroy that hierarchical order of the cosmos known as the Great Chain of Being. Until his dying day, Charles attached supreme importance to this concept. 'A subject and sovereign', he declared from the scaffold, 'are clear different things'.

The fact that his father (and sovereign), was a homosexual did not make Charles's job of coming to terms with James any easier. James had had a lonely childhood, being the shuttle-cock of warring Scots nobles, and the pupil of dour Presbyterian ministers who constantly reminded him of his mother's wickedness and her son's sins. James's homosexuality may be dated from an encounter at the age of thirteen

32 *James I* in premature old age, by Daniel Mytens. James ignored his son for pretty young men such as George Villiers, Duke of Buckingham. Mytens captures that slobbering ridiculousness, that desperate petulance, which made Charles both fear and despise his father

33 *Charles, Prince of Wales*, about 1623, by Daniel Mytens. Painted in the same year that the Venetian Ambassador described Charles as repressed by an unfortunate education, the portrait captures that youthful uncertainty which prompted him to latch on to Buckingham, and ride to Madrid in an irresponsible attempt to woo the King of Spain's daughter with his cousin Esmé Stuart. It survived Stuart's banishment by nobles (who feared his power more than his preferences), ruined James's marriage to Anne of Denmark, and may have been at the back of the Gowrie conspiracy. After his accession to the English throne the emphasis of James's sexuality changed from that of lover to parent. For instance in 1615 James began his relationship with Buckingham on a physical basis. Although he may have continued to sleep with him for several years, by 1620 the king's feelings towards his favourite had changed enough to allow him to help Buckingham wed Katherine Manners, the richest if not the fairest heiress in the land. The king took great interest in their marriage. He even visited them in their chamber the next morning to ensure the marriage had been fully consummated. He showered the Villiers clan with money and titles, creating George first Marquis and then Duke of Buckingham. He let his favourite's extensive family move into his palaces, through which hordes of their children ran like 'rabbit conies about their burrow' – behaviour the king never tolerated from his own offspring.[14] James came to think of himself as patriarch of the Villiers family, signing his letters to them as their 'dear Dad'. At a banquet in June 1618 he proposed a toast to 'that noble house of Villiers which he was determined to advance above all others whatsoever'.[15] To Charles, sitting with the king at the high table, the message was clear – if he wished to join his father's new surrogate royal family, and end his lonely childhood, he must accept a place in its cadet line.

At first Charles rejected this solution, quarrelling with Buckingham. However, in 1618 Buckingham took Sir Francis Bacon's advice that if he wanted to transfer his hegemony from one reign to the next he must cultivate the heir to the throne. By the end of the year a reliable source reported that Charles was letting Buckingham handle 'all his business of importance'.[16] In Buckingham Charles found a substitute for the older brother he had lost. His friend cushioned those feelings of immaturity that the prolonged adolescence of heirs forced to wait for a father's death often induces. Buckingham and James called him 'Baby Charles', as if he were in fact a younger brother. On their trip to Spain in 1623 Charles and Buckingham chose the aliases 'Tom and John Smith', implying that they wished to be siblings. Like a big brother Buckingham protected Charles from his father's wrath, and saved the boy from the obvious contradiction of resorting to a father figure to escape an Oedipal conflict.

By 1618, or early 1619, the triumvirate of James, George and Charles that was to dominate England's government for the next half-dozen years had been formed. Theirs was not a placid relationship, but a power struggle fought in a number of ways, some important, many trivial. We know, for example, that in 1620 Charles bet Buckingham a banquet on a game of tennis (he lost), and a little later another on which of two footmen could run the fastest (again Charles lost). However, the vast majority of such incidents, significant as part of a pattern to an analyst, were too trivial for contemporaries to record, since they considered events such as parliamentary sessions or diplomatic negotiations much more worthy of their pens. Thus it might be useful to take one such amply recorded theme, the Spanish marriage negotiations, to see what light it sheds on both the development of Charles's personality in the half-decade before he became king, and his changing relations with his father and best friend.

The origins of a marriage alliance with Spain go back to 1604, when London and Madrid signed a peace treaty ending a generation of war. First Henry, then Charles, were advanced as possible grooms for a Spanish princess, but since Madrid was more concerned with preventing an Anglo-French alliance than in making one with London, negotiations dragged on from year to year. Gradually Charles welcomed the prospect of a Spanish bride. He was irate when the 1621 parliament attacked the proposal, and warmed to the eloquent and exaggerated descriptions of the Infanta's allures from Sir John Digby, the British ambassador in Madrid. And so Charles fell in love with the King of Spain's sister – or at least fancied himself in such a state – and like a knight errant of old he decided to cut through decades of diplomatic dilly-dallying by galloping to Madrid to win his mistress in person.

In reality Charles's and Buckingham's mission to Spain in 1623 was more a farce than a romance. 'Tom and John Smith' set out on 18 February wearing false beards (that slipped about their faces), were chased by a posse near Rochester, and arrested as suspicious characters in Canterbury. They visited Louis XIII's court in Paris (while still in disguise, though with better-fitting beards), rustled mountain goats in the Pyrenees, and eventually on 7 March without warning, walked into the British embassy in Madrid to announce that they had come to take charge. Digby was flabbergasted. So was Philip IV, who responded with traditional Spanish hospitality and traditional Spanish procrastination. By May Buckingham realized

34 *George Villiers, first Duke of Buckingham*, artist unknown. This painting clearly demonstrates why Charles was attracted to his father's favourite. Buckingham was a splendidly handsome youth with piercing eyes, a cheerful smile and cherry-red lips. He had enough charm, elegance and sexual flexibility to win James's love, and then transfer his hegemony from one reign to the next, being, in effect, England's uncrowned king for a decade

35 *Charles, his family and court walking in Greenwich Park*, by Adriaen van Stalbemt. After Buckingham's assassination in 1629, and the failure to work with parliament, Charles once again retreated into his own world – that of the court. He patronized artists, poets and playwrights, collected paintings, and – as this picture shows – went for pastoral strolls. Those were, one courtier recalled, 'halcyon days'

that the Spanish were playing games, and tried to persuade Charles to return home. But he was too besotted with love to leave. 'I have seen the Prince have his eyes fixed upon the Infanta,' James Howell noted; 'he watcheth her as a cat doth a mouse.'[17] To show the depth of his devotion, early one morning Charles climbed over the wall of the garden where the Infanta took the air. As he leapt down and advanced, his lady love ran the other way, shrieking for her virtue and her chaperone, and eventually a most embarrassed prince had to be let out via a side door.[18] As Charles took charge of negotiations, the rest of his retinue became increasingly disenchanted with Spain: indeed, one of them observed that he had never believed in the Catholic doctrine of Purgatory until he had been forced to spend a summer in Madrid. As the season grew hotter the Spanish increased their demands, and the prince continued to concede. In early August, however, Philip suggested that Elizabeth's eldest son would have to marry a Habsburg before Spain could do anything about the Palatinate. Charles hardened his stance. Philip took his muted threat about having to go home soon to his aging father as a formal farewell, outmanoeuvring his uninvited guests into leaving. Eight weeks later, on 5 October, when Charles and Buckingham landed in England, the rift between the two had mended. In Spain Charles tried to act without Buckingham only to be spurned by a woman, which made him even more dependent on his male friend. During their long ride and voyage home Buckingham doubtless reminded the prince of Spanish duplicity, while their rapturous welcome to London, which was – with the possible exception of Mr Chamberlain's after Munich – the warmest ever accorded a British emissary back from a botched mission abroad, convinced them that the public would welcome a war of revenge against Madrid. Nevertheless, the king still favoured a pacific foreign policy. The complicated and tortuous shifts in Charles's attitudes toward Spain in the last three months of 1623 reveal how he oscillated between James and Buckingham. By the following spring, as the parliamentary session shows, Charles opted for his best friend. In June he boasted to the British ambassador in Paris, 'all things go well here'.[19] By the end of the year he and Buckingham completed their coup by impeaching the king's financial minister, Lionel Cranfield, and forcing James to sign a marriage treaty with the French princess, Henrietta Maria, made on terms more onerous than those rejected in Spain.

Well before Charles came to the throne in March 1625 at the age of twenty-five, his basic adult personality had been formed. It was to influence the rest of his life and reign profoundly. As we have seen, for instance, his childhood friendship with Frederick and Elizabeth, and his adolescent need for a cause, made the recovery of the Palatinate the chief goal of his foreign policy. That Charles was born a Scot, and successfully made the transition to England to be brought up among anglicized Scots, convinced him that he understood his compatriots, whom he believed would and should accept English institutions just as readily as he had. As the prayer book rebellion proved, the results of this misconception were, quite literally, fatal.

The warped relations between Charles's parents thwarted his own sexual development. Forced by James to kowtow to Buckingham he soon accepted the royal favourite as if he were his elder brother. When Charles tried to act independently of Buckingham in Madrid the results were disastrous. The Infanta's threat to enter a nunnery rather than his bed could hardly have done much to reinforce Charles's sense of heterosexual self-confidence, and enhanced Buckingham's influence enough to enable it to survive James's death, and the transition into the new reign. During the first three years of Charles's reign Buckingham in many ways ruled England. He embarked on a series of military adventures, the attack on Cadiz, the Ré campaign, the expedition against La Rochelle, that dragged England into an undeclared war with France and Spain. Being costly failures these campaigns necessitated the calling of parliament; because Charles could neither coerce nor conciliate an increasingly independent House of Commons, they produced the constitutional crisis that climaxed in the Petition of Right of June 1628.

By making Charles accept Buckingham's domination, James enhanced the authoritarian side of his second son's nature. James forced the boy to apologize publicly for his rudeness toward the favourite: once, for instance, he boxed the lad's ears for soaking Buckingham by turning on a fountain hidden in a statue of Bacchus as he walked through the gardens of Greenwich Palace. As institutions as different as English public schools and United States Marine Corps boot camps have proved, humiliation and the painful acceptance of authority, followed by the reward of the grant of authority, make the eventual exercise of that authority all the more complete. For Charles the pain of having to accept Buckingham's domination was followed by the pleasure of the duke's friendship and protection. Thus, in his turn, Charles expected – demanded – that those who defied his authority be equally contrite. He used to revise drafts of apologies from offending courtiers to make sure that they were sufficiently grovelling. The main reason why he refused to release Sir John Eliot from prison, but let the great parliamentary leader die alone in the Tower, was simply that he would not say he was sorry. Just as a benevolent father must teach his children obedience for their own good, so too must a good king instruct his subjects. And if a few recalcitrants, such as Eliot, will not learn, then they can at least serve as a lesson for the salvation of the rest.

While this model of the king as a good father served Charles badly in dealing with parliament in the 1620s and in handling the constitution and military crisis of the 1640s, it did work well during the 1630s.

Soon after Buckingham's assassination in August 1628 Charles retreated to the world of his court. He ruled without parliament. To save raising taxes he made peace with France and Spain. To enjoy his hobbies and family he left the daily routine of government to his ministers. Charles fell deeply and dependently in love with his wife. Even though they had nine children, their patronage of a courtly love cult – as exemplified by Thomas Randolph's 'Platonic Elegy', 'When essence meets with essence, and souls join in mutual knots, that's the true nuptual twine' – would suggest that the marriage of Charles and Henrietta Maria was not founded in the delights of the flesh.[20] During the 1630s Charles stayed at court, where he collected works of art, patronized poets, attended plays and took part in dramatic masques. He let his wife develop a coterie of petticoat politicians – gallants, all charming, romantic, and loyal, who would have been irrelevant were it not for the crisis of the 1640s.

Many forces helped engender this crisis: Scots national pride, English arrogance, and a widespread fear of conspiracies, especially Catholic ones. But chief among them was the king's determination that the Presbyterian Scots should use a new English prayer book, and, even more important, after they rioted against it in St Giles's Cathedral, Edinburgh, in July 1638, and signed a covenant of protest the following year, Charles's insistence that they accepted the hated liturgy no matter the cost. In reply to warnings that it would take a standing army of 40,000 English troops to make the Scots use the new prayer book, the king vowed, 'I *will rather die* than yield to the *impertinent* and damnable demands . . . of these *traitors*, the Covenanters.' The king underlined his words, the only time bar one he ever did so, to show the depth of his feelings. A number of considerations prompted him. First, Charles considered that the Scots were really republicans acting 'under pretence of religion'.

Thus he was fighting not merely for a new prayer book, but to preserve monarchy and civilized society – a laudable intention had it not been based on an utterly erroneous premise. Second, James had taught Charles to believe that as monarch by divine right, conceding to the Scots Covenanters was quite literally damnable, for by going against his conscience he would be imperilling his soul.

Realism, not self-delusion; compromise, not conscience; bargaining, not self-righteousness – these were the qualities the king desperately needed, but sadly lacked, to survive the crisis of the 1640s.

Immediately after the Long Parliament opened in November 1640 it purged the king's advisers. Archbishop Laud, Bishop Wren, and Thomas Wentworth, Earl of Strafford, were thrown into the Tower. Rather than face impeachment Secretary of State Windebank and Lord Keeper Finch fled to the Continent. Instead of accepting the new ministers chosen for him by parliament, Charles came to depend on his wife's largely Catholic and often ultra-conservative friends, who reinforced his own authoritarian inclinations, which he expressed in sudden and simple attempts to solve problems through direct action. Thus in January 1642 Charles went in person to the House of Commons to arrest the five members whom he believed had subverted the rest of parliament. Eight months later he raised the royal standard at Nottingham, declaring civil war against his rebellious subjects. As Charles learned as an adolescent, the wilful must be forced in obedience for their own good and the kingdom's happiness.

But Charles failed. Even though he fought bravely, he lost the Civil War, and in 1646 he had to surrender to the Scots. A long and complicated series of negotiations followed, first with the Covenanters, then with parliament, the army, the Scots and parliament once again, until after he had plunged the realm into a second civil war, the army decided to execute him. More than anything else it was Charles's duplicity and his inability to bargain in good faith, that signed his own death warrant. When he conceded it was always a case of too little and too late, and then at great personal emotional cost. For instance, during the negotiations with parliament at Newport on the Isle of Wight in September 1648, Charles agreed to abolish Anglican bishops and surrender control of the militia. That evening he wrote to William Hopkins, who was trying to arrange his flight to France, 'If you love my safety go on cheerfully with your preparation, for I cannot make good what I have put them in

36 *Charles I on trial*, by Edward Bower. Pastoral idylls don't last for ever, and Charles eventually found himself on trial for his life. His demeanour was dignified, yet resigned. At his trial and execution Charles defended himself well, speaking without the stutter that had bedevilled him ever since infancy hope of . . . I am lost if I do not escape.'

Once more Charles failed, and in a sense was lost. But in losing he ultimately won what he called 'the honour of a kind of martyrdom'.

Four years earlier, as he languished in the Tower awaiting his own martyrdom, Archbishop Laud had bitterly concluded that Charles 'knew not how to be or be made great'. In most respects Laud was right. In life there had been little greatness about the king. Admittedly his court was splendid, the paintings he collected were exquisite, but the tensions of his earliest years meant that Charles could not work with parliament, coordinate his Cavaliers enough to win a war, or afterwards conclude a peace. Yet in death Charles achieved a grandeur he had never known in life. It was not that the personality formed in childhood changed, rather that the demands on it altered. What had once seemed immature stubbornness now became adult resolution; obstinacy turned into courage; arrogance seemed like a sublime and mystical inner peace. From his earliest years Charles had suffered from a severe stutter, that may well have been the product of his 'unfortunate education'. But at his trial and execution he spoke without hesitation, as if death was liberating him from the tensions that had bedevilled him throughout his life.

VII

GEORGE III

'The History of the present king of Great Britain', charged the Declaration of Independence, 'is a History of repeated Injuries and Usurpations.' George III was, Thomas Jefferson concluded, 'a prince, whose character is thus marked by every act which may define a Tyrant . . . unfit to be the Ruler of a free people'. Many Englishmen have agreed. At best George was a dull eccentric who loved farming, wandered around gabbling 'What! What!' and eventually went mad. At worst he was a tyrant who, misled by wicked advisers, tried to be a king, and so usurped parliament's constitutional powers with disastrous results. 'Ignorant, narrow-minded and arbitrary, with an unbounded confidence in his own judgment, and an extravagant estimate of his prerogative' was the verdict of the eminent Victorian historian W. E. H. Lecky, who blamed the political errors of the sovereign who 'inflicted more profound and enduring injuries upon his country than any other modern English king' on a childhood and adolescence 'very unsuitable for the task he had to fulfil'.[1]

George was born at Norfolk House, London, at 7.30 on the morning of 4 June 1738. He arrived so suddenly that the only great officer of state able to get to the *accouchement* in time was the Archbishop of Canterbury. Born two months premature, the baby was not expected to survive, but (as he gratefully acknowledged some forty years later) due to the 'great attention' of his wet nurse, Mary Smith, 'my having been reared is greatly owing'.[2] When he was four a visitor described him as 'a lovely child'. The next year an artist sketched him happily reading a book under a tent that he had made for himself from some chairs and spare curtains. But three years later George's carefree childhood seems to have ended in Richard Wilson's painting of him and his brother Edward sitting awkwardly under the stern gaze of their tutor, Dr Ayscough (Plate 38). Like all the prince's tutors Ayscough had cause enough for concern, for his charge was dull, backward and apathetic almost to the point of mental retardation.[3]

George may have got his backwardness from his father, Frederick, Prince of Wales. Universally known as 'Poor Fred', he used to amuse himself by throwing stones at people's windows in the middle of the night. A contemporary thought that his chief claim to fame was as an example of how much childishness and deceit people would put up with so long as it was cloaked in the aura of royalty. Frederick's mother, Queen Caroline, hated him, often wishing her first-born dead. His father, George II, agreed. He loathed his son (and daughter-in-law) so deeply that he described their marriage as 'grafting my half-witted cox-comb upon a mad woman'.[4] Father and son fought bitterly, particularly over the latter's allowance, which Frederick tried to get parliament to double from £50,000 to £100,000. Rather than have his first child born under his parents' roof, Frederick dragged his wife, whilst in the middle of labour and at dead of night from Hampton Court to St James's Palace. No wonder Sir Robert Walpole, the prime minister who had to handle such petulance, called Frederick 'a poor, weak, irresolute, false, lying, dishonest, contemptible wretch, that nobody loves, that nobody believes, that nobody will trust'.[5]

Even so, Frederick was a fairly good father and husband, particularly by the especially low standard set by the rest of the Hanoverian kings. Notwithstanding an appetite for adultery that was as hearty as it was undiscriminating, he got on well with his wife, Princess Augusta. She was a petty German princess, from a minor German principality, whose marriage to the heir to the English throne had fulfilled her scant expectations so bountifully that she was quite content to surrender to her husband all further ambition, individuality and self-respect. Hoping for less than most, Frederick and Augusta's marriage was happier than many.

Frederick was genuinely interested in his children. He insisted that they have plenty of exercise, and stimulated his eldest son's curiosity in science and art, and his passion for farming and the theatre. But Frederick's philandering, and constant nagging that George should do more to please those about him, did nothing to enhance the boy's sense of security. Neither did his parents' obvious preference for his younger brother. 'Do hold your tongue, George. Don't talk like a fool,' they would frequently remind him.

Frederick's sudden death in March 1751 was a terrible blow. 'I feel something here,' said George, putting his hand on his heart and turning white, when Dr Ayscough told him the news, 'just as I did when I saw two workmen fall from the scaffold at Kew.'[6]

Becoming heir to the throne greatly enhanced the twelve-year-old prince's status. A month after his father's death George II made him Prince of Wales, and recommended that parliament pass a regency bill. But if his prestige improved, his lot got worse. He became lonelier. 'Silent, modest, and easily abashed,' observed Lady Louisa Stuart, 'he was a child in an adult world.' George did not like the governors whom George II appointed after his father's death. Thomas Hayter, Bishop of Norwich, was a careerist whose ambitions and advancement in the Church of England most likely came from being the bastard son of an Archbishop of York. Years later George III described him as 'an intriguing unworthy man, more fitted to be a Jesuit than an English bishop'. The king's description of his second governor Lord Harcourt, a dull but sturdy Whig, as 'well intentioned, but wholly unfitted for the situation in which he was placed', was more charitable, although just as accurate.[7]

If George had any hopes that his condition might improve after Hayter and Harcourt were dismissed in 1752 for allegedly teaching him Jacobite doctrines, he was to be disappointed. Years later George called his new governor, Lord Waldegrave, 'a depraved, worthless man'. Waldegrave had an equally caustic view of his charge, describing the boy as 'insipid', 'uncommonly indolent', 'full of princely prejudices', and inclined to pay 'too much attention to the sins of others'. In fact Waldegrave was a fairly good governor, who might have been able to do more for his pupil had not Princess Augusta dismissed him as a 'sort of pageant, a man of quality for show'.

Augusta has had a bad press – and quite rightly so. Recent attempts to rehabilitate her reputation have done little more than tax the ingenuity of her defenders. After Frederick died, leaving her a widow with eight children, and another on the way, she immediately tried to improve her standing with the king. For a time it worked. George II had her and not his younger son, William, Duke of Cumberland, appointed regent in case he died before his grandson came of age. But due to the influence of the Duke of Cumberland and the Earl of Bute relations between the king and his daughter-in-law soon degenerated to the venomous level that was the norm among the Hanoverians.

Augusta was terrified that the Duke of Cumberland, would, like some wicked uncle in a Shakespearian play, usurp the throne and

37 *Augusta, Princess of Wales, and her children*, 1751, by George Knapton. Behind George's recently widowed mother is a portrait of her feckless husband, Frederick, Prince of Wales, wearing the robes of state. Prince George is showing a plan of the fortifications of Portsmouth to his younger brother, Edward, Duke of York

38 *Prince George with his brother Edward and their tutor, Dr Francis Ayscough*, about 1745, by Richard Wilson

butcher her son. George imbibed his mother's fears. When he was thirteen, for example, on a visit to his uncle's apartment, he asked to see one of the general's fine collection of swords. Pulling one down, Cumberland drew the blade, causing the boy to turn pale and tremble, sure that he was about to be run through.

George felt more comfortable in the company of John Stuart, third Earl of Bute. Bute was born in Scotland in 1713, but from the age of ten was brought up in England. He attended Eton and Christ Church, Oxford, before being elected to represent Scotland's peers in the House of Lords. In 1741 he lost his seat in the upper chamber for opposing Walpole's peace policies, and went back to the Isle of Bute, where for the next decade he lived in as much pomp and discomfort as that beautiful yet backward island could provide. In 1746 he returned to England to try his political luck once more. Meeting Frederick at a game of cards, the two soon became friends. They shared many interests, including a passion for amateur dramatics. In 1750 Frederick made Bute one of the Lords of his Bedchamber. Bute's influence increased after Frederick's death, since he quickly filled the void left by the deceased. The scurrilous believed that as far as Augusta was concerned he did so completely:

> He busses and smacks her by night and day,
> So well does he please her, she never says nay.

Although Bute was not the princess's lover, to a large degree he became her eldest son's surrogate father. She made the earl his tutor in 1755. George responded to Bute's overtures with the same enthusiasm that gutter poets attributed to his mother. For instance, dating his letter 31 June (*sic*) 1756 he wrote:[8]

> My Dear Lord:
> I have had the pleasure of your friendship during the space of a year, by which I have reaped great advantage . . . I do therefore in the presence of Our Almighty Lord promise that I will ever remember the insults done to my mother, and never forgive anyone who shall offer to speak disrespectfully of her . . . I do in the same solemn manner declare I will defend my Friend . . . I hope my dear Lord you will conduct me through this difficult road . . . I am young and inexperienced, and want advice.

By convincing the heir that George II and his ministers were conspiring against him, Bute and his mother isolated the prince under their own control. When the king suggested the establishment of a separate household, as was usual when the Prince of Wales turned eighteen, they got him to write begging that 'His Majesty will suffer him to continue with the Princess his mother'.[9] Three years later after George II rejected the prince's request to be allowed to serve in the armed forces against the French (wrongly interpreting it as a demand to made Commander in Chief), he was outraged. 'The old king makes me ashamed to be his grandson,' George told Bute.[10] Thus when the old king suddenly dropped dead on the morning of 25 October 1760, the new one's reaction was only to be expected. 'I thought I had not time to lose in acquainting my Dearest Friend of this,' he wrote to Bute, 'and shall wait till I hear from you to know what further must be done.'[11]

Without a doubt Bute was the man who had the most influence on George's early years, and, for that matter, the whole of his life. The king admitted as much. In 1799, nearly three and a half decades after they had parted company, he called the earl 'the truest and best friend I ever had'.[12] But the influence of the king's best friend was far from wholly beneficial.

Lord Chesterfield, an enemy, described Bute as 'proud, aristocratical, pompous, imposing, with a great deal of superficial knowledge'. Prince Frederick, a friend, was even less generous, calling Bute 'a fine showy man who would make an excellent ambassador in a court where there is no business'. In a sense both were right. Bute had the makings of a fine senior tutor at an Oxford college best known for its athletic prowess. Widely if not well read, he had that peculiar blend of self-certainty and insecurity that comes to those – such as dons – who have never tested their ideas in the real world of action.

As a reminder of his father, Bute managed to play on George's emotions, as well as his intellect. For instance, in his political will ostensibly written in 1749 for his son's edification (although in fact designed to embarrass his father), Frederick had urged George to dissolve the link between Hanover and England, live with economy, and try to reduce the National Debt. Bute reinforced these views, constantly stressing the need for fiscal prudence and putting Britain first. 'Born and educated in this country, I glory in the name of Britain,' declared his student on becoming king, 'and the peculiar happiness of my life will ever consist in promoting the welfare of a

39 *John Stuart, third Earl of Bute*, by Sir Joshua Reynolds. After her husband's death Augusta depended on the Earl of Bute, who became Prince George's friend, mentor and father figure. Soon after succeeding to the throne George made Bute his prime minister. But he resigned within a year because he lacked the intelligent self-confidence that Reynolds's magnificent portrait implies

40 *George III*, by Benjamin West. Standing with the crown on one side and his soldiers and ships on the other, and wearing a soldier's red coat adorned with the order of the Garter, George seems to be the confident and contented ruler of a vast empire. Ironically the portrait was by an American

people, whose loyalty and warm affection to me, I consider as the greatest and most permanent security of my throne.'[13]

Bute was able to strengthen George's intense sense of duty and belief that true security could only be found in winning his people's love (as opposed to that of a woman), by playing on the young man's physical development.

Since he knew the gossip that Bute was his mother's lover was utterly false, the earl's role as a surrogate stepfather did not arouse any feelings of sexual jealousy in George. Paradoxically, the rumours may have strengthened Bute's influence over the boy, for had George, a most moral young man, spurned Bute, he could well have been seen as giving credence to such lies.

But George's feelings towards his 'Dearest Friend' went beyond the mere filial. One authority, writing in more reticent times than our own, described the young prince's involvement with the older man as 'a romantic attachment'.[14] George was a highly sexed youth, and there were many rumours about his affairs. There was, however, no truth in the one that he wed Hannah Lightfoot, the Quaker girl from Execution Dock, Wapping, and had several children by her before she emigrated to Australia. Notwithstanding the opportunities readily available to all heirs, if he could not marry, George preferred to burn.

And burn he did. 'I was struck by her first appearance at St. James's, my passion has been increased every time since I beheld her,' he confessed to Bute in September 1759 about Lady Sarah Lennox, who at fifteen was 'as beautiful as girl could be' – or so thought Charles James Fox. 'I am daily grown more unhappy, sleep has left me,' George went on, before protesting (perhaps too much), 'before God I never had any improper thought with regard to her.'[15]

Bute firmly quashed this passion: she was unsuitable; she was too young; she was English, and a commoner; if George did not marry a German princess, he could never inherit Hanover. Meekly the prince obeyed, dousing the flames of his ardour with a cold deluge of duty. 'The interests of my country ever shall be my first concern, my own inclination shall ever submit to it. I am born for the happiness or misery of a great nation, and consequently must often act contrary to my own passions.' Thus Bute persuaded George to divert his libidinal drives into hard work and a sense of duty. At times the king could be excessively rigid. But on other occasions he had a sense of certainty, of stability, that was to become his chief claim to greatness. 'How strong a struggle there is between the boiling youth of 21 years,' he lamented, adding that 'marriage', 'application' and keeping his mind constantly employed were the most 'likely means of preserving those passions in due subordination'. If George had to remain a virgin then at least he would be a king. Sarah on the other hand did not appear to mind that she was not a queen. She grieved more for the death of her pet squirrel, taking comfort by throwing herself at Lord Newbattle, a notorious womanizer.

A little like a doctor who gives his patient slightly the wrong prescription to ensure that his services are constantly required, Bute played on George's weaknesses. He made him feel bad so he could make him feel better. For instance, even though George's earlier tutors had all agreed that their charge was hopelessly idle, by the time he started working for Bute George was highly diligent. As his homework, now in the royal archives, proves, George worked hard; indeed, after he became king he did so almost to the point of obsession. But he always felt that he was a monster of sloth. 'I am conscious of my own indolence which none but so sincere a friend as you could so long have borne with,' he confided to Bute, who was not a good enough friend to disabuse the prince of his guilt and misconceptions.[16]

In much the same fashion Bute (and Augusta) took advantage of George's loneliness. According to Lord Chesterfield they 'agreed to keep the prince entirely to themselves. None but their immediate, and lowest creatures were suffered to approach him. Except at his levees, where none are seen as they are, he saw nobody, and nobody saw him.'[17] Thus isolated, George appreciated his captors' company all the more.

By cutting George off from the outside world they convinced him that he was surrounded by enemies. The Duke of Cumberland was out to murder him and seize the throne. All politicians must be distrusted, urged Bute, who as a young man had been forced out of the House of Lords by that consummate politician Sir Robert Walpole. George quickly agreed, complaining when he was eighteen that all the king's ministers 'have called me a harmless boy'.[18] This attitude helped Bute and George become the focus for parliamentary opposition. But since the concept of a loyal opposition had not yet fully developed, they, like most eighteenth-century opposition politicians, had to cloak their dubious stance in highly moral language. The trouble was that George and Bute believed their own rhetoric. Taught as a prince to distrust politics, as a king George III was severely hampered in his own dealings with politicians.

His attitude towards professional politicians, no matter how competent, was apparent before he came to the throne. After William Pitt, later Earl of Chatham and the hero of the Seven Years War, decided in 1758 to renew the Prussian subsidies (which protected the 'despicable little province' of Hanover at the British taxpayer's expense), George wrote to Bute, 'Indeed my dearest friend he treats both you and me with no more regard than he would a parcel of children.' George resented being told what to do by politicians, because he felt they did not treat him as a grown-up. 'A harmless boy,' he lamented, 'a parcel of children.'[19] Thus George wanted to be a king because his sense of thwarted pride, as well as his channelized libido, helped him equate it with being a man.

Less than a year after he came to the throne George wrote to Bute, 'let that mad Pitt be dismissed'. In October 1761 Pitt, the nation's most successful war leader, resigned at the peak of his triumphs. Ever since then politicians and historians have debated the constitutionality of this act. Perhaps George's real mistake was not so much one of acting unconstitutionally – for Britain's unwritten constitution was at the time particularly vague on this point – but of being ineffective. Pitt, like Winston Churchill in 1945, was a hard man to follow: except for his diffidence, Bute was no Attlee. He could not take the cut and thrust of politics. After lamenting that 'The Angel Gabriel could not at present govern this country,' he resigned in 1763. A series of prime ministers, including George Grenville, who bullied the king with cause and without mercy, followed until 1770, when George happened upon Lord North, a kindly, indolent man, with whom the king felt comfortable. But North was a disaster, who had to resign after the loss of the American colonies in 1782. George's determination to have William Pitt (the Earl of Chatham's son) as his chief minister from 1783 to 1784, in spite of repeated defeats in the House of Commons, was clearly unconstitutional, but it has not provoked the intense criticisms that his dismissal of the elder Pitt has, largely because it worked, producing stable governments for half a century.

The charge that Bute (and Augusta) brought George III up to be an absolute monarch is as erroneous as the accusation that Hayter and Harcourt taught him Jacobite principles. Bute's mistakes were letting his excessive ambitions outreach his limited abilities, insisting on his becoming a politician when he never really liked politics, and ousting the Earl of Chatham when he had not the slightest chance of eclipsing him.

To his credit, however, Bute managed to teach his pupil that sense of morality, of duty and steadfastness, that served him well throughout his reign. True, at times George could be priggishly rigid, but he often displayed a sense of stability that was a great comfort during years of intense change. An indication of Bute's achievements may be obtained by comparing George with his siblings, over whom the earl had little influence. William, Duke of Gloucester, secretly married Lady Waldegrave, the illegitimate daughter of Edward Walpole and one Mrs Clements, a milliner. Lord Grosvenor successfully sued Henry, Duke of Cumberland, for seducing his wife, after which the king's younger brother clandestinely married Mrs Horton, another widow. After being forced to marry Christian VII, the homosexual King of Denmark, his sister, Caroline Matilda, had an affair with her physician, Dr Johann Struensee, and only escaped her lover's punishment because her brother promised to send the Royal Navy to bombard Copenhagen if Christian executed her.

George had little sympathy with Caroline's conduct: the British ambassador to Denmark made him threaten to dispatch the Navy. George's willingness to buckle down and accept Bute and Augusta's authority, as evidenced by his request not to be given a separate establishment when he became eighteen, was reflected in his treatment of his own children. He and Queen Charlotte hated to see any of their six daughters leave home. Only one, the eldest, married before thirty with her parents' permission. It was widely rumoured that another, Princess Sophia, had an illegitimate child by General Garth, the king believing the story that the dropsy had made her belly swell, and the 'roast beef cure' prompted its sudden contraction! George was not so gullible as far as his seven sons were concerned. While a good father to them when they were young, as they grew older he treated them abominably. 'The king hates me: he always did from seven years old,' complained the eldest, George, Prince of Wales, who outraged his father by 'marrying' Mrs Fitzherbert, a twice-married Catholic widow. George III forced his third son, later William IV, to leave the navy even though he loved the sea, while refusing for months to let his fifth, Ernest, return home to England after he had been badly wounded fighting in his father's army. Understandably the king's sons reacted against such treatment. Like George's brothers they were not prepared meekly to accept parental authority, and so married unsuitable women, had expensively blatant affairs, gambled like fiends, and ran up enormous

41 *George III, and his family*, 1770, by John Zoffany. Surrounded by his family, George appears the embodiment of paternal happiness. As his children grew older, however, they, like all the Hanoverians, quarrelled bitterly with their parents

42 *George III at Windsor*, 1807, by Peter Edward Stroehling. Here the king looks rather like a gentleman farmer, with his estate in the background and an adoring spaniel at his feet. It was this commonsensical ordinariness which helped stabilize England in a time of extraordinary change debts, becoming, as the Duke of Wellington fulminated, 'the damnedest millstone about the neck of any government that can be imagined.'

The duke exaggerated. With their peculiar sense of logic the public found the instability of those close to the royal family a reassuring reminder of the worth of a stable, albeit stodgy, sovereign (just as later the scandal of George IV's divorce suit against Queen Caroline, with its lurid allegations of her midnight trysts with a coachman in Italy, may have distracted public discontent away from the social problems caused by the Napoleonic wars. The damnedest millstones facing George III's government were not the king's sons, but his colonies in North America.

In this crisis George's inflexibility revealed itself clearly. He told Lord North in 1774 that the passage of the act virtually suspending the Massachusetts charter 'gives me infinite satisfaction. Four months later he concluded that 'the die is now cast, the colonies must either submit or triumph'.[20] But the king was not directing British policy in North America. He was merely performing the monarch's constitutional duties that Walter Bagehot defined as to be consulted, to encourage and to warn. Thus in 1766 George rebuffed the Duke of Bedford's suggestion that he take the initiative regarding the repeal of the Stamp Act by replying, 'I do not think it constitutional for the crown personally to interfere in measures which it has thought proper to refer to the advice of parliament.'[21]

King George became the bogeyman of the Declaration of Independence not because he was a tyrant (although he was an enthusiastic supporter of policies that Jefferson considered tyrannical), but because the common sense and decency that he conveyed reinforced in many colonial minds a concept of the monarchy that was no longer valid in England.

Eight years before he signed the Declaration of Independence Benjamin Franklin called George III 'the best king any nation was ever blessed with'.[22] That same year the Boston town meeting, quite rightly recognizing that their quarrel was not with the king, passed a motion condemning the 'taxes raised from them by the Parliament of Great Britain'. Patriots believed that once the king learnt of parliament's conspiracy against their freedoms as Englishmen (albeit resident on the other side of the Atlantic), then 'the paternal care of the best of sovereigns' would, as one of their pamphlets put it, rescue 'his loving subjects in North America'. Theirs was an archaic concept of the king as *pater patriae*, as head of a family that extended throughout the cosmic order, and which the revolution of 1688 had rendered obsolete in England. Thus it is not surprising that it was an Englishman, Thomas Paine, resident in the colonies but three months, who shattered the fantasy that George was the good father eager to save his dutiful children. Once *Common Sense* convinced Americans that George was really 'the royal Brute of Britain', and not the 'loving father of your whole people', a new myth, equally false but far more damaging, emerged.

At worst George's part in the American Revolution was as the ardent supporter of a misbegotten policy. At best his denying Roman Catholics the right to vote after the 1801 Act of Union merged the Dublin parliament with that in Westminster, was the block-headed adherence to a misinterpretation of his coronation oath. Even though George had sworn to protect the established church, his refusal to permit Catholic emancipation did nothing to safeguard Anglicanism, while infecting Anglo-Irish relations with a poison still felt today. From this charge, and not his culpability regarding the American Revolution, the excuse that he was mad is most relevant and necessary. Pitt did not insist on emancipation in 1801 as strenuously as he might have, since he feared this might induce another of the king's attacks.

Apart from the problem of Catholic emancipation, and the unseemly scrambles for the regency by the Prince of Wales and his political cronies, politically George's madness was not so important. After all he was fifty when he experienced his first bout, being deranged for no more than six months in the first seventy-three years of his life.

During the night of 17 October 1782 George suddenly fell ill with stomach cramps. Within a few days the symptoms grew far more disturbing. According to Queen Charlotte his eyes became 'nothing but black current jelly, the veins on his face were swelled, the sound of his voice was dreadful, he often spoke till he was exhausted . . . whilst foam ran out of his mouth'.[23] The following month George had to be strapped into a straitjacket, his doctor, the Reverend Francis Willis, being convinced that madmen must be broken like horses. Dr Willis's poultices of Spanish fly and mustard raised blisters on George's thighs while doing nothing to cure his fantasies that he could see Hanover through the astronomer William Herschel's telescope, nor abate his rambling sexual fantasies concerning Lady Elizabeth Pembroke. Despite everything the finest medical minds of the day could do to him, George recovered. In April 1783 he resumed

43 *George III in old age*, artist unknown. The contrast between this and the previous portrait could not be greater. This painting shows a Lear-like mad king, abused by his family, tortured by his doctors. Recent research has proved that porphyria, a genetic defect, made him seem insane his duties, although with less energy and concern for detail than before. He suffered a relapse twelve years later in 1801, and a third attack in 1804. By the time of his fourth bout George was blind, deaf, and virtually senile. A regency had to be established, and George III lived his last decade a mad, sad, Lear-like prisoner in Windsor Castle.

The cause of the king's derangement baffled his doctors, and has occasioned much debate ever since. It has been attributed to an Oedipal complex, to his frustrations at not being able to have his way, either with the American colonies or Lady Pembroke. Others have blamed his madness on repressed guilt for having married and then deserted Hannah Lightfoot, or on the strain of having to make love to so ugly a woman as Queen Charlotte. Even though Charlotte was not the prettiest of ladies, one courtier ungallantly observing that middle age had ameliorated 'the *bloom* of her ugliness', there is no evidence that he performed his marital duties with reluctance.[24] Far from it: as her husband grew older Charlotte tried to protect herself by insisting that at least one daughter remain in her bedroom.

Recently a new and conclusive explanation of the king's madness has been advanced – that he suffered from porphyria, a rare genetic disease not identified until the 1930s. George had the classic textbook symptoms: port-red urine caused by too much red pigmentation in the blood, that also produces the brain disorders and the incessant activity, uninterrupted speech, delusions, fantasies and violent outbursts that he displayed. George was not the first of his line to suffer from porphyria. Mary Queen of Scots, James I, Prince Henry, Princess Henrietta Anne, Queen Anne (Charles I's brother, daughter and granddaughter, respectively), all displayed symptoms. So did four of George's sons, as well as his sister, Caroline Matilda, and his granddaughter Princess Charlotte.

But unlike most porphyria victims George did not die young. He lived until the age of eighty-two, passing away on 29 January 1820. Two days later he was buried in St George's Chapel, Windsor. 'And thus has sunk into an honoured grave the best man and best king that ever adorned humanity,' wrote Mrs Arbuthnot in her diary after attending the funeral, 'who for sixty long years had been the father of his people.'[25]

She was right.

George's reign saw revolutionary changes that swept not just the realm, but the whole of the known world – the Industrial Revolution, the French and American Revolutions, the first British embassy to China and the first settlements in Australia, a defeat in America unknown since the loss of England's French possessions nearly half a millennium before, and a world war against Napoleon not to be repeated until the catastrophe of 1914–18. Even though at times he was deranged, quarrelled with his children, supported ineffectual ministers, could be infuriatingly stubborn and, as with Catholic emancipation, terribly wrong, George managed to retain an ordinary sense of decency. He communicated it to the old rural squires and the new industrial entrepreneurs who were the backbone of a rapidly changing England. He could talk to them about those mundane subjects that often form the strongest bonds between men. He would stroll the lanes of Gloucestershire chatting to farmers about the price of wool, publish papers on new crop techniques, under a readily recognized *nom de plume*, or simply walk the streets of Worcester without a bodyguard, passing the time of day with ordinary folk. 'Few have laboured harder at being a good king than George III,' Prince Charles has written. 'He cared and he was a genuine, honest person; qualities which quickly endeared the king to all classes of his subjects.'[26] With all his faults, problems and troubles, George's earliest years served him well. Rather than producing the last active English king, who tried to turn the clock back to Stuart despotism, they helped foster the first constitutional monarch, who hesitatingly, and with many a misstep, blazed the trail that his granddaughter Victoria was to pave, and that his direct descendant, Prince Charles, has astutely recognized.

VIII

VICTORIA

It is one of the best-known scenes in the history of the British monarchy, the long-awaited death of an old king, the early morning visit of grave counsellors to a young, untried girl. Painted by contemporaries, described by biographers, memorized by generations of schoolchildren, the story is still best told by its central figure. On the evening of 20 June 1837, she wrote in her journal:[1]

> I was awoke at 6 o'clock by Mamma who told me that the Archbishop of Canterbury and Lord Conyngham were here and wished to see me. I got out of bed and went into my sitting room (only in my dressing gown), and alone, and saw them, Lord Conyngham (the Lord Chamberlain) then acquainted me that my Uncle, the King, was no more, and had expired at 12 minutes past 2 this morning and consequently I am Queen.

Victoria's first day as as queen was an extraordinarily busy one. In it she both set the themes for her sixty-three-year reign, the longest in English history, and revealed many of the strains engendered by a difficult childhood and adolescence. She ordered that her bed be removed from her mother's room, where she had slept since birth, to a chamber of her own. Had she been able to do so, she would have dismissed Sir John Conroy, her mother's adviser and best friend, or sent him as governor to some distant, disease-ridden colony. At nine on the first morning of her reign she had an audience with her prime minister, Lord Melbourne – 'alone', as she pointedly noted in her diary. Immediately she fell under the spell of this charming father figure. A little later she presided over the first meeting of her privy council, enthralling statesmen all old enough to be her father. 'She not merely filled her chair,' recalled the Duke of Wellington, 'she filled the room.'[2]

Had the duke been able to read her diary entry for that night he would have been even more delighted. 'I will do my utmost to fulfil my duty toward my country,' vowed the queen. Commitment and an intense sense of responsibility were among her most appealing virtues, as were honesty and self-awareness: 'I am very young, and perhaps in many, though not all things, inexperienced but I am sure that very few have more good will and more real desire to do what is fit and right than I have.' Throughout her life Victoria wanted to serve and be served, to be dominated and to dominate, to be subject and sovereign. Ultimately the latter prevailed. 'I delight in this work,' she confessed less than twenty-four hours after her coming to the throne had liberated her from an almost unbearable upbringing.[3]

Victoria was born on 24 May 1819 in Kensington Palace, the first and only child of an improbable union. Her parents had married reluctantly for pragmatic reasons in 1818, before falling in love with a surprising warmth. Two years earlier Princess Charlotte, the Prince Regent's only child, died in childbirth. Her husband, Prince Leopold of Coburg, was as stunned as the nation. Now there seemed to be no clear heir to the throne. The Prince Regent hated his wife, Caroline, with such a passion that there was no chance of the two ever producing another child. Most of his younger brothers had either married contrary to the Royal Marriages Act or else were believed to be too happily ensconced with mistresses of many years' standing to produce legitimate heirs. Edward, Duke of Kent, George III's fifth son, had been living with Madame de St Laurent ever since she was introduced into his house and bed when he was a young officer at Gibraltar twenty years before. She followed him to Canada where he was posted for punishing the troops with barbarous severity. She stayed at his side after he muffed his second chance and was dismissed as Governor of Gibraltar in 1801 for flogging the garrison into mutiny. The duke was, quite simply, an unhappy, sadistic martinet who combined a vicious nature with a little mind – 'the greatest rascal that ever went unhung', thought the diarist Charles Greville. Madame de St Laurent loved him, staying with him even after the auditors appointed to discharge his appalling debts insisted that he leave England for Brussels, where the cost of living was much lower. There they remained, a contented, middle-aged couple, until one morning in 1816 when the duke carelessly handed to her across the breakfast table a copy of the latest *Morning Chronicle*, which urged the duke to cast aside his trollope, marry, produce a legitimate heir, and so earn the gratitude, as well as the increased allowance that the

44 *The Duchess of Kent with her daughter, Victoria*, aged three, in 1823, by Sir William Beechey. Having never known her father, who died when she was one, Victoria was exceptionally close to her mother

nation bestowed on those who served it during times of need. After a painful scene, Madame de St Laurent left the breakfast table, and the duke's life, to live in graceful retirement in Paris, whilst he continued the courtship that he had been secretly pursuing for the past couple of years.

The duke's new love was far less accommodating than the old one. Princess Victoria of Saxe-Coburg had had a hard life. In 1803, at the age of seventeen, she married Charles, Prince of Leiningen, a widower twenty-three years her senior who neglected her to spend his days hunting. He died in 1814, leaving Victoria with two children, Charles and Foedera. Widowhood came as a relief. Having been denied any part in running Leiningen, as Princess Regent Victoria desperately needed help. She latched on to Captain 'von' Schindler, an ambitious courier, who purloined the aristocratic prefix to enhance his status as Master of the Household and of the Horse. When the Duke of Kent first proposed marriage to the princess 'von' Schindler objected; she would lose her independence, perhaps custody of her children – and he his influence. Anyway the duke was a bully and deeply in debt. Victoria declined. Princess Charlotte's death, and the possibility that her child might inherit the British throne, quickly changed her mind, and she married the duke at Kew on 13 July 1818.

Ten months later Victoria was born on 24 May 1819. Influenced perhaps by the Romantic movement, the duchess insisted on breast-feeding the baby herself (which probably makes Victoria the first English monarch who was not put out to a wet nurse). 'She was so unmanageable that I nearly cried,' the duchess wrote to her mother after taking her month-old daughter outside for the first time. 'To my shame I must confess that I am over anxious in a childish way with the little one, as if she were my first child: she drives me at times into real desperation.'[4]

Other problems beset the new mother. Even though parliament had increased his allowance the profligate duke was still desperately in debt. In November 1819 he decided to leave London for Sidmouth in Devon, where the cost of living was lower and the climate healthier. In the New Year the duke caught a fever. Having survived the tropics and the arctic wastes, the fifty-two-year-old veteran met his match in the finest medical men of the day. After they had bled him copiously, he died on 23 January. 'He was the adored partner of my life,' lamented his widow. 'Whatever shall I do without his strong support?'

The effect of her father's premature death on Victoria is hard to ascertain. Although she was too young at seven months even to remember him, there is no doubt that Victoria spent much of her life looking for a father figure.

She found her first substitute father in Leopold of Coburg, her mother's younger brother, who had married the late Princess Charlotte. 'What a happiness it was for me to throw myself into the arms of that *dearest* of Uncles, who has always been to me like a father, and whom I love so very *dearly!*' the sixteen-year-old princess effused to her journals when he came to visit her in September 1835.[5] A year later, during another visit, she used Italian – perhaps to hide from herself the depth of her feelings. 'He is indeed "il mio secondo padre" or "solo padre". For he is indeed like a real father, as I have none.'[6] Leopold was one of the cleverest politicians of his day. Genuinely fond of his niece, while being astutely aware of the advantages of cultivating the heir to the British throne, he sent Victoria a stream of excellent advice. She should establish a regular routine for reading state papers and seeing ministers. She must not make hasty decisions, for once taken they would be hard to retract. Leopold helped Victoria survive the crises of adolescence which were made even more painful by the strictures imposed by her mother and Sir John Conroy. When his duties as King of the Belgians prevented him from coming over to England in person he sent his trusted adviser, Baron Stockmar, instead. 'He is one of those people who talks plain honest truth, don't flatter, give wholesome necessary advice,' wrote Victoria about the baron. 'I feel so towards him.'[7] Perhaps the greatest service her uncle did her was persuading Victoria to marry his nephew, Albert, and then letting Stockmar remain in England to help turn their idyllic marriage into a constitutional triumph.

The second father figure Victoria found also helped in this process. 'It had long been my intention to retain him and the present ministry at the head of affairs,' Victoria wrote of Lord Melbourne on the first day of her reign, adding, 'I like him very much and feel confidence in him.' At the age of fifty-eight Melbourne was still a very handsome and witty man, and for the next four years he served as the queen's prime minister, chief tutor and best friend. If he infected her with his own conservative, even reactionary, indifference towards the poor and unfortunate, as well as his dislike of 'bother', he at least showed a ill-prepared girl how a monarch should behave. Doing so brought great happiness to a lonely old man who had known little

45 *Victoria aged about eleven*, by Richard Westall. A charming portrait of a seemingly carefree young girl

46 *Sir John Conroy*, after A. Tidy. Conroy was an unscrupulous Irish adventurer who inveigled himself into the duchess's confidence in order to control the young heiress to the throne

joy. After a notorious affair with Lord Byron, his wife, Lady Caroline Lamb, went mad, dying in 1828. Their only child, a feeble-minded epileptic, followed her a year later. 'I have no doubt he is passionately fond of her,' Charles Greville observed of Melbourne's feelings towards Victoria, 'as he might be of his daughter if he had one; and the more because he is a man with a capacity for loving without anything to love.'[8]

Victoria's feelings towards Melbourne were more complicated than she would admit even to her journal. 'He has something so fatherly and so affectionate and kind in him that one must love him,' she confided in 1838.[9] A superb raconteur, he opened up vistas for the young queen, telling her the latest gossip, laced with sophisticated yet cynical observations about a host of subjects ranging from wife-beating, doctors, the French, the Irish, to bringing up children. He made her feel part of an extended family with his endless stories about her predecessors, George II, George III, George IV, her uncle William IV, and her father, the Duke of Kent. 'From all I have heard,' wrote the relieved young woman, not realizing that the competition was far from keen, 'my father was the best of all.' Victoria drank it all up, finding Melbourne's company a heady brew. As Charles Greville observed, 'Her feelings, which are sexual, though She does not know it, and are probably not very well defined to herself, are of sufficient strength to bear down all prudential considerations.'[10] Melbourne was more than a father figure. He represented the first love – often platonic, sometimes more – that young women frequently feel towards older and wittier mentors. Constitutionally this love served the nation well. Emotionally it was of great value, for it repaired her battered psyche for the adult commitment of marriage.

Casual observers thought that Victoria had been a happy little girl. After meeting the nine-year-old princess at Kensington Palace, Mrs Arbuthnot, the Duke of Wellington's confidante and thus no mean judge of character, wrote that she 'is the most charming child I ever saw. She is a fine, beautifully made, handsome creature, quite playful and childish playing with her dolls, and in high spirits.'[11] But an aunt who knew the princess better recalled that when she was six she would go around exclaiming to herself, 'Poor Vicky, she is an unhappy child.'[12]

Her daily routine seemed ordinary enough. Up in time for a breakfast of bread, milk and fruit at eight, then riding for an hour, playing with her toys, lunch at half past one. In the afternoons she might do lessons with her mother and then go out for a drive or walk, before dinner at eight and bed at nine. Most of the time she and her mother lived in reduced circumstances, the Duke of Kent having left them nearly penniless. They had to depend on the generosity of Prince Leopold, whose civil list allowance of £50,000 continued even afer Princess Charlotte's death. Not until 1830 did parliament grant £10,000 a year for Victoria's education. She passed most of her childhood in Kensington Palace. Every summer she, her mother and Conroy would rent a house for a month at Ramsgate, where Victoria would play on the beach. Although it was a sensible regime Victoria's childhood failed to provide an affectionate girl with any outlet for her feelings, except for her rather stern German nanny, Louise Lehzen, and her collection of 130 wooden dolls, and did nothing to prepare her for the rigours of 'The Kensington System', which she entered at about the age of ten.

Charles Leiningen, Victoria's older half-brother, recalled that the Kensington system had three goals. The first was to make Victoria popular by distancing her from, and thus contrasting her with, the old king in the hope of making the heir to the throne a focus for the opposition, as happened with the Hanoverians. The second goal was to ensure that if the king died before Victoria reached majority her mother would become regent, and the third was that if the king passed away after Victoria came of age at eighteen she would make Sir John Conroy her permanent private secretary.

The éminence grise behind the whole scheme was an unscrupulous adventurer from Connaught. Conroy had a certain Irish charm and a familiarity with the ladies that many found vulgar. 'God! I don't like this man,' observed Melbourne on their first meeting, 'there seems to be something very odd about him.'[13] Baron Stockmar agreed, warning the Duchess of Kent that Conroy was 'vain, ambitious, most sensitive and most hot tempered'.[14]

Conroy was born in 1789 and commissioned in the Royal Artillery at the age of seventeen. An ambitious captain, he married the only child of Major General Fisher, a good friend of the Duke of Kent. After avoiding action during the Napoleonic Wars, he entered the duke's household, only to be disappointed by his patron's premature death. He worked his charm on the duchess, whom he may have reminded of 'von' Schindler, the adventurer on whom she had leant after losing her first husband. Certainly Conroy played on her fear that the Duke of Cumberland might murder her daughter and seize the throne, and her resentment at the royal family's neglect. Always in debt, ever eager for an increase in her allowance, a foreigner with few friends in a alien land, the duchess was sensitive to every slight, ignoring Stockmar's warnings that Conroy was 'the sole regulator of the whole machine'.[15]

In one respect, however, Conroy had little influence. Victoria's education was left to tutors. The first was the Reverend George Davys, Fellow of Christ's College, Cambridge, who taught her French, German, music, and history. The schedule was pretty light, two hours of class in the morning and two in the afternoon. Victoria learnt enough to impress a board of bishops whom the duchess asked to examine her in 1830. Perhaps they had scant expectations of a ten-year-old girl, for in later life Victoria admitted, 'I had benefited but little from what I had learnt.' While she sketched well and sang sweetly, and admitted that 'Reading history is one of my greatest delights,' her formal education did not challenge the fifteen-year-old who told her uncle Leopold, 'I love to be employed; I hate to be *idle*.'[16] Instead it left her woefully ignorant of maths and science, and feeling inadequate in the company of intellectuals.

Conroy pressured Victoria emotionally rather than intellectually. Even though his relations with the duchess were platonic, Victoria may have believed the gossip that they were lovers. When she was eleven Conroy engineered the dismissal of Baroness Spaeth, her mother's lady-in-waiting, of whom Victoria was most fond. A little later he tried to have Louise Lehzen, Victoria's beloved governess, dismissed. Although he failed, and Lehzen remained to protect her charge from the worst of Conroy's excesses, Victoria soon lost another protector. 'I sobbed and cried violently the whole morning,' she wrote in her journal after her half-sister, Foedera, left home to get married; 'I loved no one better than her.'[17]

Pressure from Conroy increased as Victoria grew older and closer to the throne. She became next in line upon the unlamented death of George IV in 1830. 'There was never an individual less regretted of his fellow creatures,' declared *The Times*. Victoria thought his successor, her uncle William IV, 'odd, very odd and singular',[18] When she visited him she would flatter the kindly old man. She was bitterly hurt when her mother (and Conroy) used some slight over precedence as an excuse – which *The Times* called 'indecent and offensive' – to boycott the new king's coronation. 'Nothing could console me,' she wrote; 'not even my dolls.'[19]

In order to enhance Victoria's popularity Conroy insisted that she go on tours about the country. These progresses outraged the king, who was fully aware that Conroy wanted to contrast the hopeful young heir with the aging incumbent, and was irritated when the duchess demanded many of the honours, such as the firing of salutes, reserved for the sovereign. Victoria disliked these trips. Even though they enhanced her knowledge of the people over whom she would one day rule, she hated Conroy's company. The strain of arduous journeys along rutted roads damaged her health. Indeed, the emotional pressure on the young woman was so intense that Stockmar wondered if at eighteen she was physically capable of marriage. During the autumn of 1835, while on holiday at Ramsgate, Victoria fell dangerously ill, possibly from complications resulting from severely infected tonsils. Conway and her mother used the opportunity to try and make her sign a promise that on becoming queen she would appoint Sir John her private secretary. Physically weak, and emotionally alone – apart from Lehzen – she drew upon the last reserves of courage to refuse.

Matters reached another crisis two years later. Realizing that he had not much longer to live, on 18 May 1837 William IV proposed that when Victoria became eighteen in six days' time parliament should vote her an allowance of £10,000 a year to set up her own household. The duchess and Conroy were outraged, the latter threatening, 'If the princess will not listen to reason she *must be coerced.*' This time they prevailed, telling Victoria that she was still too young and owed everything to her mother's care and love. The princess surrendered, writing back to the king, 'I wish to remain as I am now, in the care of my dear Mother,' to whom she requested the £10,000 allowance be paid. A few days later Victoria came of age. 'How old!' she wrote in her journal, 'and yet so far I am from being what I should be.'[20]

Victoria was far closer to her goal than she realized. Within three weeks her uncle died, she became queen, and her mother's and Conroy's machinations were utterly foiled.

Even so, the pair had an indelible effect on Victoria's personality. 'I was extremely crushed and kept under,' she wrote, 'and hardly dared say a word.' Her hatred of Conroy was total and permanent. Whenever men tried to bully her in a similar fashion she resisted with the same stubbornness she had shown at Ramsgate. When Sir Robert Peel (whom she thought 'such a cold odd man') insisted that he appoint all her ladies-in-waiting as a condition for forming a new Tory ministry in 1839, Victoria refused. 'They wished to treat me like a girl, but I will show them that I am Queen of England,' she

47 *Victoria holding her first privy council meeting*, by David Wilkie. Wilkie deliberately altered Victoria's dress from black to white to show the innocence of a young queen surrounded by experienced men all old enough to be her father

48 *Queen Victoria out riding with Lord Melbourne*, by Sir Francis Grant. Between Victoria and her first prime minister developed a touching father–daughter relationship that lasted until her marriage to Albert in 1840. Not only did Melbourne help her assume the burdens of an office for which her mother had ill prepared her, but his teachings laid the foundations for today's constitutional monarchy

49 *Inauguration of the Great Exhibition in 1851,* by Henry Selous. The Great Exhibition expressed Britain's overweening pride in the achievements of the age that we still call Victorian. This portrait of the royal family flanked by British and foreign dignitaries conveys the majesty of the ruler of the world's most powerful nation. At the same time it stresses the virtues of domesticity, and warm family life, that appealed to the new middle classes who were the entrepreneurs of Britain's greatness exulted, delighted that in spite of his defeat in the Commons she could now ask Lord Melbourne, a Whig, to return as her prime minister.[21] Victoria's relations with her sixth premier, Lord Palmerston, were equally strained. 'I *never* liked him,' she wrote of this stern, domineering man.[22] She positively loathed William Gladstone, complaining that he would address her as if she were a public meeting. Never one to hide his erudition, Gladstone made the queen painfully aware of the inadequacy of her education.

While the bully in Conroy revolted the queen, the *outré* in this swashbuckling Irish adventurer somehow fascinated her. Conroy was the anti-father figure, and his portrait suggests a more than passing resemblance to her real father. Perhaps Victoria inherited this infatuation with the *outré* from her mother. Even though she used this adjective as one of reproach in her journal, the outlandish clearly intrigued her. On reading Washington Irving's *The Conquest of Granada* at the age of sixteen she recorded her first fascination with the mysteries of the East: 'These are all Phantom Castles which I love to form.' The same year she confessed in her journal to feeling a delicious thrill on seeing the notorious Duke of Brunswick. As a young woman she was enthralled by Uncle Leopold, with his extravagant wigs, three-inch platform shoes, feather boa, rouged cheeks and blatant makeup. As a married woman on a state visit to France in 1855, she was delighted when Napoleon III outrageously made love to her, tickling her vanity without touching her virtue. As a widow she satisfied her fascination with the *outré* in her long friendships with Benjamin Disraeli and John Brown.

Two more different men would be hard to find. One was a charming, silky, anglicized Jew, with visions of Empire abroad, the other a rough, even crude Scot, whose horizons stretched scarcely beyond his native Highlands, and his sovereign's most immediate services. But both, in their very different and complementary ways, were the queen's intimates at roughly the same time.

On first meeting Disraeli in 1844 she thought him 'unprincipled, reckless and not respectable' – all adjectives she would gladly have applied to Conroy. After Disraeli became her prime minister for the first time in 1868 their relations quickly grew close. No longer the radical novelist who had condemned the social inequities of British society in *Two Nations*, Disraeli was a mellow, lonely widower who begged the queen to 'deign not to withhold from him the benefit of your Majesty's guidance'. Trowel-loads of extravagant flattery worked. 'When one's husband is gone, and one's Children are married – one feels that a friend, who can devote him or herself entirely to you is the one thing you do require,' wrote the queen. Just as Lord Melbourne had led Victoria out of her childhood, so Disraeli brought her out of the valley of the shadow of Albert's death. As well as being a father figure, Disraeli inveigled the queen back into the mainstream of the nation's life by dangling before her a bazaar full of eastern delights that included the Suez Canal and the title of Empress of India.

John Brown embodied that simple utter loyalty that India's first English empress treasured from all her subjects – black, brown, and white. A ghillie from the Highlands, he served his monarch with the clansman's honest unquestioning (and unquestioned) fealty to the chief of his clan. Good-looking, intelligent, strong, and undoubtedly brave, he first came to the queen's attention in Scotland as the excellent coachman who saved her from several potentially nasty riding accidents. Victoria's doctors brought him south to Osborne House on the Isle of Wight in October 1864 to cheer up the widowed monarch. Soon he became her personal servant through whom courtiers, ministers, even her children, had to go to reach the sovereign. Tongues wagged as usual, suggesting that the two were secretly married. Far from it. Brown served the queen with honest respect not servility. She found his transparent devotion touching, his weakness for a dram amusing, and his gruff familiarity – 'Hoots there, wumman, can ye noll hod yerr head up' – proof certain of sincerity. On his death in 1883, two years after Disraeli's, she said, 'He became my best and truest friend – as I was his.'[23]

No one, not even Abdul Karim, was able to fill the place of Disraeli and Brown. She doted on Abdul, the son of an Indian jail apothecary, whom she made her Munshi. Her obvious favour and complete lack of racial prejudice upset courtiers and ministers, who resented the mysterious Muslim less for the scant influence he had over the queen than for the colour of his skin. Little known to the general public, Abdul Karim was the last *outré* figure in the queen's long life. As she grew older she developed a new public image, that of the matriarch both to her own people and to Europe's extended royal families.

Victoria's relations with her own mother provided little help in this transformation. On ascending the throne she immediately spurned the Duchess of Kent, moving her bed from her mother's room. The duchess, 'a duck who had hatched forth a swan, whom she adored, but never understood', was deeply hurt. 'This was

50 *Victoria visits Disraeli at his house, Hughenden*, etching by an unknown artist. Albert's death devastated Victoria. For decades she remained a recluse, the 'Widow of Windsor' whose neglect encouraged the growth of republicanism. But another father figure, the dashingly romantic politician Benjamin Disraeli, coaxed her out of mourning to shape the modern monarchy

51 *Victoria and three future kings, Edward VII, George V, and Edward VIII.* By the
end of her long reign Victoria had become the matriarch of most of Europe's royal
families. The theme of four generations that is captured in this photograph was a
popular one. Taken at Edward VIII's christening, it promised dynastic continuity.
Within half a century, however, two world wars destroyed England's hegemony,
forcing its royal family to adapt to a very different world

neither a happy nor a merry day for me,' she lamented on her birthday soon after her daughter's accession. 'Everything is so changed.'[24] To vent her feelings about ungrateful daughters, she gave Victoria a copy of *King Lear* for her nineteenth birthday. The animosity was mutual. 'I don't believe Ma. ever really loved me,' Victoria confided to Melbourne at about the same time.[25]

Instead she found a substitute in the woman she called 'dearest Mother Lehzen . . . the greatest friend I ever had'. The daughter of a German pastor, Louise Lehzen came to England as Foedera's governess, becoming Victoria's in 1824. 'She devoted her life to me,' recalled the queen, 'with the most wonderful self-abnegation, never ever taking one day's leave.' Every night Lehzen would sit up with Victoria until she fell asleep. She provided the security and affection the young girl craved, shielding her from the extremes of the Kensington System. Unable to dismiss her, Conroy mercilessly teased Lehzen about her provincial German habits (including incessantly eating carraway seeds to control flatulence). In the end Lehzen and her charge won. She, more than anyone else, helped turn a bullied child into a great monarch. Queen Victoria was the first to acknowledge this debt. On hearing of Lehzen's death in 1870 she said, 'She was an admirable governess, and I adored her, though I also feared her.'[26]

Victoria's ambivalence towards Lehzen was reflected in the change in her feelings towards her real mother. Time healed many of the scars. Having children of her own taught Victoria – as it does us all – to be more charitable of her own parent's failings. Long before the Duchess of Kent's death in 1861 the two were fully reconciled. Going through her mother's papers afterwards, Victoria realized how much the duchess had really loved her, Conroy's schemes notwithstanding.

But Victoria did not learn how to avoid her mother's mistakes with her own children. As Prince Albert told her in 1856, 'It is indeed a pity that you find no consolation in the company of your children. The root of the trouble lies in the mistaken notion that the function of a mother is to be always correcting, scolding, ordering them about, and organizing their activities. It is not possible to be on happy, friendly terms with people you have just been scolding.'[27] Victoria's (and Albert's) relations with Edward, Prince of Wales, proved the sagacity of the Prince Consort's advice, for they were notoriously bad. She blamed her eldest son – rather than Windsor Castle's typhoid-riddled drains – for her husband's death. Even though she and her eldest daughter, Vicky, carried on a long and intimate correspondence after the princess left England to marry Prince Frederick William of Prussia, Victoria made no secret of her dislike of pregnancy and childbirth. As she wrote to Vicky, who relished motherhood, 'I think much more of our being like a cow or dog at such moments.'[28] Like her own mother Victoria did not want to let go of her children. 'A married daughter I MUST have living with me,' she insisted.[29]

By and large Victoria's rejection of the Duchess of Kent's and Conroy's influence was politically beneficial, allowing a far more sensible man, Lord Melbourne, to shape the start of her reign. But in one respect, at least, it had adverse consequences. Victoria hated Lady Flora Hastings, her mother's lady-in-waiting, who during her illness at Ramsgate had joined the duchess and Conroy in trying to force her to make Sir John her secretary. Thus when in 1839 Lady Flora's belly started to swell the queen happily believed the malicious stories that she was with child, almost certainly by Sir John, with whom she had shared a post chaise on the way back from Scotland. Distraught, Lady Flora insisted on being examined by the royal doctors, who reported that she was still *virgo intacta*, but, mindful more of their careers than of the ethics of their profession, added that this did not invariably preclude pregnancy. In fact Lady Flora had cancer, which caused her death in July. Even though the queen made a half-hearted apology, her popularity plummeted so precipitously that she was hissed whilst out riding. Clearly it was time for her to find someone who could mitigate the excesses engendered during her youth.

The partnership between Victoria and Albert was one of the most creative in the evolution of the British crown. It had an intensity, a passion, that was a far cry from the grandiloquence of the Albert Memorial, which the heartbroken queen built to commemorate her husband. Albert was exceedingly handsome, appealing to Victoria's weakness for good-looking males. He neatly complemented his wife, his childhood being happy. He liked mathematics, science, was serious, sexually faithful and utterly understanding. At times his wife could be difficult, almost to the point of neurosis. She vented her feelings on him in a way she had never been permitted to do as a child or adolescent. Indeed, it sometimes seemed as if the tension bottled up in earlier years, where even her diary was read and could not serve as a true safety valve, came exploding out during her tantrums with Albert. He responded with thoughtful, reasonable letters to his 'Dear Child'. While Victoria might well have preferred a more masterful male who, like Brown would have slapped her down with a 'Shut up, wumman!' she loved her husband for his deference to her as his sovereign, and his authority as the peerless paterfamilias. Albert satisfied Victoria's need to dominate and be dominated. He was everything to her: father, lover, counsellor, guide, protector, husband, father of her children; he even, she admitted, gave her 'Motherly love'.

So when Albert died prematurely in 1861 and Victoria returned to the void created by her early years, she was devastated: 'I have lost my guide, my support, my all.'[30] She became a recluse, she neglected her public duties, while continuing to draw her civil list. *What Does She Do With It All?*, one of several pamphlets, asked if she gave fair return for her annual parliamentary allowance, while throughout the land republicanism grew to heights unknown since Cromwell's day.

The Prince of Wales's almost fatal illness of 1871 saved the monarchy. The public could empathize with a mother's fears as she worried for the life of her son, and they for the nation's future. When Edward recovered her joy was theirs. Thanks in large part to Disraeli's influence, the queen came out of a decade of mourning triumphantly to become the nation's mother figure. A generation and two royal jubilees later, in 1900, a London policeman told the crowds who noticed the royal standard flying above Buckingham Palace, 'Mother's come 'ome.' Three years afterwards, on learning of the queen's death, Marie Corelli, the popular novelist, acknowledged, 'She was our Mother.'

Royalty had changed. While it had ceased to be a political force well before Victoria came to the throne, during her reign it found a new role. Indeed, the absence of such a part left a vacuum, making the reigns of her predecessors, George IV and William IV, almost an interregnum in the history of the crown. Victoria founded the modern monarchy by making it into a symbol for the nation, and the empire's hopes, aspirations, fantasies and mundane worries. She did so by blending the ordinary with the extraordinary, the everyday with the unattainable. Ever since portrait painters had depicted the young queen wearing a white dress for her first privy council meeting (Plate 47) instead of the historically correct black one, Victoria became the focus for her subject's emotions. What stern nineteenth-century male heart would not melt in loyal pride at the sight of Susannah out riding with the elders? As a wife and mother she stressed the virtues of middle-class family life that appealed to the new men of the Industrial Revolution. They needed a symbol of British commercial superiority as self-confident as the Great Exhibition of 1851; so too did they crave for signs of their own dynastic worth as comforting as Albert's Christmas tree, or Dickens's *Christmas Carol*. Even the excesses of Victoria's widowhood struck a sympathetic note with a people who were all too painfully familiar with death, and (as the success of Little Nell demonstrated), wallowed in its prolonged extravagances. The Prince of Wales's recovery struck a similar chord, although this time *fortissimo*, since it had a happy ending. It let the Widow of Windsor become India's Empress and Britannia's ruling Mother. In her person she combined both distance and intimacy, that sense of being unattainably different, yet, in her family especially, identifiably the same as her subjects. This has become part of the familiar mystique of the modern monarchy. Like many important changes in history it took place without deliberate intent, almost by accident. Unlucky in her childhood, lucky in her husband and ministers, desolate in widowhood, fortunate in her son's recovery, Victoria became the matriarch who seemed to have been ever there, a sure bastion in an uncertain world of change. Victoria did not just found the modern constitutional monarchy, she helped turn the royal family into the ideal and mirror for her people.

IX

EDWARD VIII

Very early on the morning of Saturday 12 December 1936, Edward, Duke of Windsor, was driven into Portsmouth Naval Dockyard. Less than two days earlier he had signed the Instrument of Abdication giving up the crown. 'I have taken this, the most serious decision of my life,' he told the world in a BBC broadcast on the evening of 11 December, because 'I have found it impossible to carry the heavy burden of my responsibility and to discharge my duties without the help and support of the the woman I love.' Now, a few hours after his radio broadcast, he was being driven into exile and ignominy. As they arrived at the dockyard his chauffeur took the wrong gate so he had to reverse the car and enter the one where a guard of honour was waiting. Then, as they drove past Nelson's flagship, HMS *Victory*, Edward turned to Sir Walter Monckton, the trusted adviser sitting beside him, and said, 'I think Nelson would have understood what I am doing. He too loved – loved *deeply*.'[1] They went up the gangway of HMS *Fury*, where Edward kept the officers up drinking in the wardroom until two that morning, when reluctantly he gave permission for the destroyer to weigh anchor for France.

Somehow it all seemed typical of the man and his brief reign: the wrong gate and the wrong woman; the lack of consideration for those who served the crown; the massive and fatal ability to deceive himself. Admiral Nelson would never have approved, for he, like millions of the subjects of a modern constitutional monarch, expected Englishmen to do their duty.

'The History of Edward VIII', the king's leading biographer has rightly observed, 'is the history of an Abdication.'[2] And the history of the abdication is in many respects the history of Edward's childhood and earliest years.

In one regard the origins of the abdication go back even before Edward's birth on 23 June 1894. Three years earlier Queen Victoria had selected Princess Mary of Teck as the bride for her eldest grandson, Prince Eddy, Duke of Clarence. The following May the dissolute duke died, leaving his sober younger brother, Prince George, next in line of succession after his father, and thus in need of a wife. Victoria considered several candidates before she concluded that Eddy's late fiancée was still the most suitable. Mary and George were married on 6 July 1893. They had much in common. Both were painfully shy and undemonstrative, with a stern sense of duty. For a couple with little expectations of happiness, or capacity for it, theirs was a surprisingly successful marriage. But as parents both were resounding failures.

George and Mary failed, for instance, to supervise their children's nursery properly. Edward's first nanny was a possessive sadist, who would twist his arms or pinch him so that he would burst into tears on being presented to his parents in their drawing room every night before bed. Hastily they would hand the bawling infant back to his nanny's noxious care. Her hatred was equally venomous. She disliked Edward's younger brother Bertie (later George VI) so intensely that she fed him sporadically, giving him the stomach ulcers from which he suffered for the rest of his life. When Edward was three his nanny, who had never been given a day off work, had a nervous breakdown, and, with her identity charitably hidden from posterity, she was dismissed from the royal service, having done incalculable harm to her charges. Edward's second nanny, Mrs Bill, was at least not malevolent, although she never became an affectionate mother figure to be adored in retrospect.

More significant in the boy's development was Finch. A handsome, utterly loyal man, without a trace of servility, his father having been in the Duke of Wellington's household, Frederick Finch first entered royal employment as a nursery footman. He shined Edward's shoes, laid out his clothes, drew his bath, making sure he washed behind his ears, nursed him when sick, and even knelt beside him each night as he said his prayers. Finch, who went on to become Edward's valet, admitted that at times he found his royal charge 'a handful'. Once, after Edward had particularly upset Mrs Bill, Finch grabbed the eight-year-old lad by the scruff of his neck, dragged him to his room, threw him on the bed, and applied his massive hand to that part of the anatomy that Victorians were convinced the Almighty had specially created for the chastisement of children. Edward threatened to tell his parents and have Finch dismissed. But when they heard of the incident, and his threats, they forced him to go and apologize personally to the servant. Told of the incident in later life, Edward denied all memory of it, confessing that he must have erased it from his mind as too painful to retain, since Finch was an honest man who could not possibly have made it up.[3]

There was no way that Edward could have forgotten the efficacy of his chief tutor, Henry Hansell. 'Looking back over those curiously ineffectual five years under him,' he said, 'I am appalled to discover how little I really learned. I am today unable to recall anything brilliant or original that he ever said.'[4] It was probably the precise lack of these qualities, which Edward's father neither possessed nor regarded with anything more than the deepest distrust, that attracted Prince George to Hansell. A bachelor, educated at Malvern College and at Magdalen College, Oxford, Hansell combined a little learning with that muscular Christianity which the Victorians seemed to associate with a love of hearty exercise and the incessant smoking of evil-smelling pipes. Prince George had chosen Hansell as his son's tutor more for his abilities as a golfer and yachtsman than as a schoolmaster. Painfully aware of his shortcomings, Hansell urged the prince to send his sons to a good preparatory school, rather than force them to attend the cramped room at York House, Sandringham, which had been fitted up with blackboard, desks, and texts, almost as a parody of real education. Hansell had only one intellectual passion, a love of ecclesiastical architecture, which prompted him to drag his reluctant charges round every church and cathedral he could find. He failed, however, to engender in his pupils the slightest passion for pulpits, gargoyles or flying buttresses. Edward developed a marked distaste for the Anglican religion and its churches, having not the least interest in art, architecture or culture. Only after Prince George discovered to his horror that his sons could not add up the weight of the stags he had slaughtered during a day's hunting did he hire a tutor to teach the boys mathematics. Edward hated his French teacher, Mlle Dussau, a strict disciplinarian who constantly informed his parents about his misdeeds, and he came to despise French as 'an effeminate language', much preferring German instead.

'I had a wretched childhood,' Edward recalled as an old man, 'of course there were short periods of happiness, but I chiefly remember it for the miserableness I had to keep to myself.'[5] The only instructor he remembered with any warmth was Walter Jones, the Sandringham village schoolmaster, a natural teacher, who communicated to his royal charges a love of nature whenever he filled in for Hansell

52 *The royal children with their father at Sandringham, 1902.* Edward is in the centre, with his brothers Bertie (later George VI) (left) and Henry (right) and his sister, Mary. The princes' tutor, Mr Hansell, is second from the left

during the tutor's vacations. Thus when the royal family moved to Marlborough House in 1903, the nine-year-old Edward found the noise and restrictions of London particularly irksome. During his childhood, he was lonely, and yet never alone. He was constantly surrounded by his brothers and sister, nannies, and servants, and yet he had no real friends. The football games that Walter Jones organized with the village schoolboys turned out to be painful episodes of bruised shins and a bruised ego. There was no one with whom Edward could share the rough and tumble, the joy and pain of boyhood. Instead, as he admitted, 'Growing up for me was a prolonged misery.'

His father's decision to send him to the Royal Naval College at Osborne in 1907 did not improve things in the least. The Naval College, housed in Queen Victoria's former residence on the Isle of Wight, combined the philistinism of an English public school with the Royal Navy's traditions of brutality. Bullying was covertly encouraged. One of the house captains publicaly flogged his son, a cadet, with the whole college, including a medical officer, in attendance. In his first term the thirteen-year-old prince had red ink poured over his hair, and on another occasion his neck was jammed into a window as a painful reminder to one of Charles I's descendants of what the English people did to kings who displeased them. The cadets were forced to jump out of bed at six every morning, into a cold bath. They were forced to get dressed fast, sometimes in less than thirty seconds – clearly an impossible goal, failure to achieve which meant punishment – before running to breakfast. The food was atrocious, and everything was done on the double. Having been poorly prepared by Hansell, Edward found the college's emphasis on mathematics and science particularly difficult, and he never came close to the top half of his class.

Even though his father had confidently boasted that the Navy would teach his son 'all he needs to know', Osborne did the boy little good.[6] The discipline was harsh. While it might have taught his classmates to lead convoys to Murmansk, or even sink the *Bismarck*, it was no help in producing a constitutional monarch. As George VI observed, his elder brother 'never had any discipline in his life'. Osborne failed to produce that strength of character whose absence Noël Coward noted when he remarked cuttingly that Edward had 'the charm of the world, with nothing to back it up'.

After two years at Osborne Edward was relieved to be able to move up to the Royal Naval College at Dartmouth. After he took a three-month graduation cruise as a midshipman aboard HMS *Hindustani* in 1909 he admitted, 'I enjoyed the experience immensely.'[7]

For Edward happiness proved transitory, particularly where his father was concerned. After the captain of the *Hindustani*, an old shipmate, told the king, 'I would never recommend anyone sailing a ship under his command,' George V decided to send his eldest son to Oxford.[8] He chose Magdalen, partly because it was Hansell's old college, and because its president, Sir Herbert Warren was a terrible snob, who had selected its junior common room for its pedigree rather than for any academic potential or performance. Edward did not want to go to the university. He confided to Lord Esher, 'I am not clever, not a bit above the average.'[9] He told his father that he was not interested in learning and that his years at Oxford would be utterly wasted,

The prince, at least, kept his word. Painfully shy, poorly prepared, he was a mediocre student whose intellectual performance may well have suffered from being tutored by some of the best minds (and most intimidating personalities) the university had to offer. If the purpose of sending Edward to the university had been to enable him to mix with gentlemen of his own sort, to get coaching in foreign languages, and to learn something about the British Constitution, Oxford had some success with the first two goals, and was an utter failure with the third. Few thought him much of a college man. Edward irritated his fellow undergraduates by playing the bagpipes in his rooms late at night. Even though he gave a few dinner parties, except for Walter Monckton, he made no lasting friends. He played tennis and golf, enjoyed beagling and riding with the South Oxfordshire Hunt. He played on his college's second football eleven, and joined the Officer Cadet Corps, where he reached the rank of corporal. In all Edward found Oxford 'a dreary bore', leaving the university after two years, without a degree, and with no apparent regret on either side. 'Bookish he will never be,' was Sir Herbert Warren's charitable verdict.[10]

Warren also noted another aspect of the prince's personality that flowered during his time as a student, his 'natural dignity and charm'. It came to the fore during his vacations when he visited his relatives in Germany. He enjoyed these trips tremendously, going for a flight with Count Zeppelin, and visiting the Kaiser in Berlin. They engen-

53 *Edward, Princess Mary, Prince John and Queen Mary visiting the Crystal Palace in 1911.* Edward is wearing a naval cadet's uniform. He hated Osborne Naval College, with its discipline, spartan life, and stern sense of duty

54 *Edward entering Magdalen College, Oxford, 1912.* As an undergraduate Edward found Oxford 'a dreary chore', having neither the aptitude nor the application for intellectual pursuits. His energies and charm found outlets on the tennis courts, golf links, and following the beagles

dered a life-long infatuation with Germany. 'I admired the industry, the perseverance, the discipline, the thoroughness and the love of Fatherland.'[11]

None the less when the First World War broke out in August 1914 Edward, like so many of his generation, was eager to fight for his country. At the time, he was an officer in the First Battalion of the Grenadier Guards and was bitterly disappointed when his unit was posted to France without him. 'It was a terrible blow to my pride, the worst in my life.' He begged Lord Kitchener, just appointed Secretary of War, for permission to join his battalion at the front. 'What does it matter if I am killed,' he insisted, 'I have four brothers.' The problem, Kitchener explained, would not be if he were killed but if he, as heir to the throne, were taken prisoner.[12]

So Edward had to settle for a staff officer's appointment behind the lines. He inspected the troops, raising their morale, trying whenever he was allowed to share their dangers. On one occasion shrapnel killed his driver when Edward was touring forward positions. The men said that whenever the shelling was at its worst the Prince of Wales would appear. Disdaining a staff car, which would splash mud on tired infantrymen as they stood in the ditches to let it pass, Edward rode miles on a standard army issue bike, always with a smile or a wave for those soldiers he met, seeming never to forget a name or a face. 'He was the most charming and delightful human being that I had ever known,' recalled a fellow officer.[13] Posted to the ANZAC Corps in Egypt in 1916, he won the regard of Australian and New Zealand troops not normally predisposed towards pommie officers, and was equally popular with the XIV Corps in Italy the following year, and with the Canadians with whom he ended the war in France.

Like many of his generation, Edward came of age during the First World War. He embraced the values of the men in the trenches. No postwar visit of the Prince of Wales, be it to a Black Country slum or to some small settlement in the Australian outback, was complete without an inspection of the local ex-servicemen's organization. Time and time again Edward would recognize someone, saying, 'The last time I saw you was outside Armentières or on the Menin Road.' Feeling intensely guilty at not being allowed to fight in combat – unlike his younger brother George, who manned a gun turret at Jutland – Edward identified with the ordinary soldiers, scorning the empty patriotism of his father's generation, who had stayed safely at home to gorge themselves on war profits and bellicose propaganda.

The war convinced Edward that he understood his generation, and they lionized him as one of their own.

But the war left him feeling ill at ease. He had never been in action: he had never proved himself in the same way as had those who cheered him. Thus for much of the period after the war he deliberately courted danger. He went steeple chasing, until his father told him to stop after he fell off and was knocked unconscious for several hours. So Edward took up flying. On going solo he never piloted a plane again, for flying was not so much a sport as a virility test.

Peace confirmed the popularity that Edward first found in wartime. For a dozen years he toured the world, being welcomed everywhere with that hysterical enthusiasm usually reserved for matinée idols or pop singers. He went to Canada and the United States in 1919, to Australia and New Zealand the following year, to India in 1921, to Africa and South America in 1925, back to North America in 1924 and 1927, and to Africa in 1928 and again in 1930, returning to Latin America a year later. These tours were great successes, doing much to enhance British prestige, sell British goods, and strengthen the bonds of the British Empire. 'Tell Daddy that we are all happy under British rule' read a sign put up, presumably by the natives, when he visited Aden in 1921.

But as time went on Edward tired of the adulation. He lost interest, he grew petulant, becoming more and more unpunctual. One day he wrote in his diary, 'What rot and a waste of time, money and energy, all these state visits are!' Once Edward doffed his charm he revealed that there was very little underneath. While he resented being denied entrance into the world of power that he thought surrounded the sovereign, he hated the demands on his time, energies and scant sense of duty that would be made of him when he actually became king. Edward was both anxious to inherit, and fearful of what his father's death might bring. After a game of polo he threw down his helmet, exclaiming to an aide, 'Oh God, I dread my father dying. I dread the thought of becoming king.'[14]

As his son grew older George V increasingly shared this view. When Edward was born his father noted in his diary, '22 June 1894. White Lodge, Richmond Park. At 10.0 a sweet little boy was born, and weighed 8 lb.'[15] George tried to do his best for Edward. 'Now you are leaving home, David, and going out into the world,' he assured the lad on the train as he was taking him to Osborne to join the Naval College, 'always remember that I am your best friend.'[16] In fact his father was his worst enemy. An extraordinarily reserved

55 *Edward during the First World War inspecting the Gas School at Helfaut, France, with his father, 1917.* Edward complained that George V put him 'always on parade, a fact that he would never let us forget'. His diffidence in his father's presence is obvious from this photo, which may also convey some of the deep resentment he felt at being forced to gallivant with the staff behind the lines instead of fighting with the men at the front

56 *Edward in America, 1919.* Edward liked Americans for their openness, and his visit immediately after the war was a great success. Smiling, cheerfully puffing a cigarette, naval cap at an angle, he conveys much of the jaunty charm that Admiral Beatty or Franklin D. Roosevelt exuded, and which made him so popular with ordinary folk both at home and abroad

man, he had to admit to problems in dealing with his offspring. 'I am devoted to children, and good with them,' he once remarked, 'but when they grow up you can only watch them go their own way and can do nothing to stop them.'

Without doubt George V was the most significant figure in Edward's life largely because he tried to stop him from growing up, and he succeeded – with catastrophic results. Quite simply Edward was obsessed with his father. In his memoirs, *A King's Story*, he wrote:

> I have often felt that despite his undoubted affection for all of us, my father preferred children in the abstract, and that his notion of a small boy's place in the adult world was summed up in the phrase 'children should be seen and not heard'. It was once said of him that his naval training had caused him to look upon his own children much as he regarded noisy midshipmen when he was captain of a British cruiser – as young nuisances in constant need of correction.[17]

King George was a martinet who bullied his children with the lack of mercy typical of those who sincerely believe that they are acting from the highest motives. His second son, George, stuttered painfully, perhaps as a result of his father's attempts to break him of being left-handed. Edward was constantly nervous, always adjusting his tie or pulling his shirt cuffs straight. Both sons smoked far too much. 'It calms me,' Edward explained. It also killed him, for Edward VIII died of cancer of the throat, while George died of lung cancer.[18]

Naturally Edward tried to hide his feelings towards his father. Only to cronies would he admit in an unguarded moment, 'My father does not like me,' adding, after a few more drinks, 'I'm not at all sure that I particularly like him.' Publicly Edward revealed his feelings about his father most openly in a slight book he wrote in 1960, entitled *A Family Album*. Unlike his memoirs *A King's Story*, a ghost-written bestseller which reputedly earned the duke a million dollars, it is hard to see why he wrote *A Family Album*. Most likely he did so for money. It starts as a family history, laced with a few revealing confessions: 'Always on parade . . . we had a bottled up childhood.' 'Being my father's eldest son I bore the brunt of his criticisms.' 'It was not easy to please my father.'[19] After a few pages he turned the book into a history of court fashion, with attack after attack, as bitter as they were oblique, upon his father. An extraordinarily ordinary man who never had an original thought in his life (a criticism that he would have regarded as the highest praise), George V constantly criticized the way his son dressed. When the young man appeared wearing turn-ups on his trousers, the king asked the Prince of Wales if it had flooded outside. Why else would a gentleman roll up his trousers except to paddle? He insisted that his children pull their socks up over their knees when wearing shorts. He reprimanded Edward when he saw photographs showing him wearing the incorrect medal ribbons on his uniform during the First World War. Afterwards he would reprove him in the harshest quarter-deck voice for the slightest infringement of the royal dress code: 'You dress like a cad, you act like a cad. You are a cad. Get out!'

Edward rejected far more than the way his father dressed. George V had an almost fanatical sense of punctuality. Edward was notoriously tardy. 'Unlike my father,' he wrote, 'I myself have never tired of travelling.' He recalled how his father, for whom he used to caddy at a shilling a round, refused to teach him and his brothers golf. 'If we let those boys on the fairway, they would only hack it up,' George explained.[20] In later life Edward became a keen golfer. Characteristically, he blamed his father for his excessive swing, and had the balls he played in his three holes-in-one (two more than Ben Hogan had ever made, he used to brag) specially mounted for the mantlepiece in his study. Unlike his father, who disliked Americans and was proud of the fact that he had never set foot in the land of informality and new ways, Edward loved the United States and its people. He had first tasted the full joys of success independent of his father during his trip there in 1919.

As George V grew older he recognized that he had failed with his heir. He urged the boy to marry some sensible girl who would make something of him, just as Bertie had settled down with Lady Elizabeth Bowes-Lyon. Had Edward done so, his relationship with the king might have improved – as his brother's had. The king once told his second son and his favourite daughter-in-law (one of the few people who ever stood up to him) how easy it was to work with them, since they were always ready to listen to his advice and accept his opinions. All 'very different', the king concluded, from his eldest son.[21] To his prime minister George was even more frank. He told Stanley Baldwin that he wished to God that somehow Bertie and Elizabeth could inherit and their children after them, rather than

Edward. 'After I am dead the boy will ruin himself in twelve months,' the king said gloomily.[22]

Edward fulfilled his father's prophecy with seven weeks to spare.

The new king started his reign badly. On 20 January, as his father lay dying at Sandringham, Edward ordered all the clocks in the house to be put back half an hour to Greenwich Mean Time. Of course, having them fast, as had been Edward VII's and George V's practice, was hardly logical, saving little daylight in January. But calling the clocksmith out of bed to put them right in the middle of the night, even before his father was dead, displayed neither sensitivity nor consideration for others. The next day Edward went to London by plane, creating 'a kingly precedent', he proudly recalled, 'for my father had never flown in his life'. He also created a poor impression at his first privy council meeting. Clement Attlee remembered that Edward looked 'very nervous and ill at ease', and that Stanley Baldwin told him he doubted if the new king would 'stay the course'. Neville Chamberlain shared the prime minister's concern, writing in his diary that if Edward VIII did not 'pull up his socks he will soon pull down the throne'.[23]

For the next few months the king seemed to disprove their fears. He made a good first speech to his people over the radio and acquitted himself bravely when a deranged journalist tried to shoot him during the Trooping of the Colour ceremony. But disturbing hints soon appeared. He neglected ministers' advice, even trying to initiate foreign policy. He soon tired of reading the incessant red boxes of state papers, becoming so careless of their contents, returning them weeks late, often with what appeared to be cocktail glass stains on them, that the government feared for their security. Indeed, for the first time ever, the Foreign Office started censoring the most sensitive documents it sent the sovereign. During the summer Edward chartered the luxury motor yacht *Nahlin* for a well-publicized cruise down the Adriatic, and across the Aegean to Turkey. He and his companion Mrs Simpson were seen swimming together, walking hand in hand, dining in seaside taverns, obviously in love, as the crowds cheered and the world's press lapped it up. Only the British newspapers ignored the story, failing to mention Mrs Simpson or else airbrushing her out of photographs which were printed showing the king alone on vacation. They dammed the scandal for months, until so tremendous a head built up that when the news broke in England the tidal wave carried the king before it.

Edward abdicated because he wanted to marry Mrs Simpson no

matter what the cost. He did so for emotional and constitutional reasons, many of which went back to his earliest years, having a great deal to do with his father.

Constitutionally the issue at stake in the abdication was simple. It was not whether the King of the United Kingdom, of the Empire and the Dominions, should be allowed to marry a twice-divorced socialite from Baltimore with both husbands living, but whether a constitutional monarch had to accept the advice of his ministers. It was not a matter of who was right, but who in a democracy should prevail. The leaders of the Labour Party, who feared what an active king might do to them if they formed a government, were particularly adamant. As the trade union leader J. H. Thomas told Harold Nicolson (later George V's official biographer), ' 'ere we 'ave this obstinate little man with 'is Mrs Simpson. Hit won't do 'arold. I tell you that straight.'

Under George V the monarchy had changed, coming to stand not for flashy cleverness or superficial charm, but for solid, even boring integrity. Edward VIII scorned the crown's dignity with what he liked to think of as openness, and modern honesty. He did not realize that the British people would tolerate all manner of sins from their sovereigns, including Victoria's excessive mourning, Edward VII's extravagant appetites, George V's boring ordinariness, so long as the crown did not make a fool of itself. Edward VIII became ridiculous, prompting sniggers that the monarch who had once been an Admiral of the Fleet now preferred to serve as third mate aboard a Baltimore tramp.

The king naturally saw his actions in a very different light, arguing that 'What was at stake, of course, was the question of my right to make a life on the Throne in terms of my own philosophy.'[24] Thus without his ministers' encouragement he made friendly overtures to Nazi Germany, and as Prince of Wales had roundly criticized the leaders of the London County Council for refusing to allow Army Cadet Corps in the schools they controlled. When the Foreign Secretary, Anthony Eden, suggested that the king should invite the recently deposed Emperor of Ethiopia, Haile Selassie, to Buckingham Palace, Edward demurred, saying that it would offend the Italians. Edward was probably right when he declared that 'something should be done' about the intolerable economic conditions in the Welsh valley, but he was certainly wrong to suggest that a constitutional monarch should take the initiative in doing it. 'Behind all this lay an important, if concealed difference of opinion between my Ministers and me,' he explained, without comprehending that in a democracy, founded on the principle of one man, one vote, a king, chosen by the accident of birth, cannot be allowed to differ from the politicians the people have elected to power.

Edward was emotionally unsuited to the role of constitutional monarch. Having no real friends, and having inherited his father's advisers, whom he automatically distrusted, he had no one to teach him the limits of his authority. Edward was a superficial man. Charming on the surface with little underneath, he could not accept that a modern monarch was very much a similar illusion. The moment he believed the pomp of monarchy, the rhetoric of the national anthem, that the crowds cheered Edward the man and not the monarch, then nothing – not even God – could save the king.

Claiming to modernize the monarchy, he was in fact putting the clock back by centuries not a mere half-hour. Having disliked London since the age of nine he spent much of the time leading up to the abdication not fully in touch, a couple of hours away at his retreat, Fort Belvedere, near Virginia Water in Surrey. Having been forced to write a weekly letter of at least six pages to his parents from Osborne, Edward hated routine paperwork, one of the crucial duties of a modern monarch; a letter in his own hand is most rare. 'Being a monarch', he recalled, 'in these egalitarian times can surely be one of the most confining, the most frustrating, and, over the duller stretches, the least stimulating jobs open to an educated, independent-minded person.'[25] Edward preferred charm to diligence, simple solutions to complex answers. Having been forced, superficially at least, to bow to his father's authority, Edward in his turn became distinctly authoritarian. As an observer noted in 1936 the king wanted to go 'the dictators' way', and is pro-German, against Russia, and 'against too much slipshod democracy'.[26] Twenty years after the end of the Second World War that had revealed the Führer as far more than the bulwark against Bolshevism who built the Autobahns, Edward told an intimate, 'I never thought Hitler was such a bad chap.'[27]

Such remarks revealed a man almost incapable of learning, who, to compound it all, had been poorly educated. Mr Hansell, for instance, had explained the 1905 election by cutting out pictures of Sir Henry Campbell-Bannerman and Arthur Balfour, the Liberal and Conservative party leaders, from a newspaper, and moving them up a ladder as the votes came in. No wonder the king came to despise politicians, particularly during the abdication. He invariably thought of Stanley Baldin as some malignant squat being who would come, unwelcomed, into his life in a car that always reminded him of a black beetle. Nostalgically he wrote of how Queen Victoria would make her ministers face the difficult, often stormy, journey across the Solent to the Isle of Wight, to see her. 'He felt he was being coerced like a wilful boy', was how the Duchess of Windsor later explained her husband's feeling towards his ministers. 'This infuriated him'.

Once more Edward blamed it all on his father. He described the changes he made on George V's death as those of 'an educated independent-minded person' who was only trying to replace the stuffiness of his father's court and generation, by throwing open the windows to let in fresh air. Edward was not the first veteran of the First World War to feel this way. Many other ex-servicemen donned black, brown, or blue shirts, to find an easy solution to the crisis of the 1930s, without their judgments being clouded by the pangs of love.

There cannot be the slightest doubt about the intensity of Edward's feeling towards Wallis Simpson. His youngest and favourite brother, Prince George, described him as 'besotted with infatuation'.[28] His best friend, Major 'Fruity' Metcalfe, thought, 'It's very pathetic. Never have I seen a man more madly in love.' 'The king is insane about Wallis,' recorded 'Chips' Channon, 'insane.'[29]

The first woman in Edward's life, his mother, disliked motherhood intensely. She found childbirth 'a complete violation to one's feelings of propriety'. Queen Mary never understood her firstborn. 'What a curious child he is,' she once remarked. Her shyness erected a barrier between herself and her children that Edward could never cross. 'We talked a lot but of nothing very intimate' was how he once summed up a meeting with his mother.[30]

On the surface he remained very fond of her. As a man, during his world travels he carried a photograph of her in a silver frame which he set beside his bed. In his memoirs he was never openly critical of her. While he recorded that as a boy he dreaded the summons to his father's library, 'a small cheerless room', for some stern reprimand, or, even more disconcerting, a friendly chat of rather forced heartiness, he relished his mother's warmth. He wrote, 'Just as my mother's room came to represent a kind of sanctuary at the end of the day, so the Library became for us the seat of parental authority, the place of admonition and reproof.'[31] In fact he fantasized. Neither his mother, nor the nanny who loved and then pinched him, nor Mrs Bill, ever gave Edward the security he craved as a child, and which as a man he sought elsewhere.

As a boy growing up in the crowded nursery at York House, his grandparents' home, Sandringham House, a few minutes walk and yet a world away, seemed to be, he recalled, a place of 'perpetual sunlight'. Edward VII and Queen Alexandra spoilt him and his brothers and sister, letting them stay up late, playing games with them, and allowing them glimpses of an excitingly raffish world, that included the king's mistress, Mrs Keppel. When his parents went off on a world tour to Australia in 1901 their children went to stay with the king and queen. They had a grand time. Finding Mlle Bricka's French and German lessons a bore, they persuaded their grandfather to leave her behind in London when the royal party went to Sandringham. A greater contrast between his parents and grandparents would have been hard to find. It seems clear that Edward VIII identified with Edward VII, and perhaps even with his late uncle – and mother's erstwhile fiancé – Prince Eddy. He recalled, 'My grandfather began, from his earliest youth, to do the wrong thing in the critical eyes of his father, and mother.' We can speculate whether he might even have wondered what would have happened had Prince Eddy lived to become his father, and make him a very different person – perhaps one he would rather have been. We do know, however, that when he became king he took the significant step of adopting the name Edward, instead of David, the one his parents and family used.

Although both King Edwards were womanizers, there was a marked difference in their attitudes towards women. Edward VII consumed them as he did food, relishing quality as much as if not more than quantity, with a hearty, even healthy gusto. The sight of the monarch with a pretty woman in tow provoked not jealousy from the crowd, but cries of 'Good old Teddy!' Edward VIII's appetites, and thus the public's reactions, were very different. An abstemious eater who preferred a light lunch of fruit, there was something neurotic about his affairs. Apart from the casual one-night stands, which passed unrecorded as mere *droit de seigneur*, Edward was seriously attracted to only two *unmarried* women, Rosemary Leveson-Gower, the Duke of Argyll's daughter, and Audrey James, daughter of an American industrialist and an English mother (widely rumoured to have been one of Edward VII's mistresses). After sensing Prince Edward's attention both women quickly married, although they and their husbands remained on good terms with him.

Edward preferred married women. He seems never to have been jealous of their husbands, past or present, or their lovers, cherished or spurned. As one such husband, Ernest Simpson, said, Edward never really grew up; he remained a Peter Pan. 'He never', concluded Mrs Dudley Ward, 'quite came to full bloom.'

All four of the great loves of Edward's life were married women who were, as Mrs Simpson put it, 'very much like a man in many ways'.[32] During the First World War he fell in love with Lady Rosemary Coke, twelve years his senior, to whom he poured out his heart in long and passionate letters from the Front. Amused and flattered, she may have taken his virginity and accommodated his passions with that gentleness and absolute discretion typical of the bored wives of English aristocrats, who had been faithful long enough to produce sufficient legitimate heirs.

In May 1918 Edward found a new love, quite literally bumping into her. As he was walking through Belgrave Square one evening the sirens went, and he took refuge from the raid in the house of Maud Kerr-Smiley (who was, by chance, Ernest Simpson's sister). Here, in the cellar, as the Zeppelins flew overhead, and the ack-ack guns barked, he fell in love with Freda Dudley Ward. That night he used ten exclamation marks to tell his diary that he had just met the most beautiful, wonderful girl in the world.

Freda was married to the Right Honourable William Dudley Ward, a Liberal MP and Vice-Chamberlain of the Royal Household, who spent far more of his time in the House of Commons than with his wife and their two children. For the next sixteen years Edward was abjectly in love with her, visiting her every day he was in London, telephoning her incessantly, acting as uncle to her children, showering her with presents, and in return demanding a paramour's passion and a mother's warmth. To be sure, Edward was not completely faithful, and Mrs Dudley Ward, like a good mother, did not seem to mind. He had numerous brief affairs, particularly during his royal tours, where the wives and daughters of crown servants seemed only too anxious to be of service to the crown. He had a five-year affair with an American beauty, Thelma, Lady Furness, Gloria Vanderbilt's sister, who had married the shipping magnate Viscount Furness when she was only twenty.

All of Edwards mistresses, whether casual or more committed, realized the limits and privileges of their positions. Mrs Dudley

57 *Edward VIII visiting the* Queen Mary *at Clydebank, 1936*. Forbidden to serve with the troops during the war, Edward desperately wanted to identify with ordinary working men, particularly during the Depression. Because he was charming, and seemed to care for them far more than the politicians, they (like these cheering workers from 'Red Clydeside') responded with great enthusiasm

58 *A bored Edward VIII at a debutantes' garden party at Buckingham Palace, 1936*. When forced to perform official duties Edward admitted to a 'thunderous boredom', obvious from this photograph. This did nothing to endear him to the Establishment

59 *Mrs Dudley Ward on a bicycle*. Debutantes interested Edward far less than did their mothers. Because he had never resolved his feelings towards his own mother, he repeatedly fell for older married women. Mrs Dudley Ward filled the role of royal mistress with tact and devotion

60 *Edward and Mrs Simpson at Balmoral.* Having being through the divorce courts twice, Mrs Simpson amply satisfied Edward's penchant for married women. As an American she also possessed that nation's informality, which Edward found so attractive, as well as its ignorance of monarchy, which was to prove so fatal. Reared on the Declaration of Independence she thought that the King of England could do what he willed

61 *The Duke and Duchess of Windsor in Germany to visit Hitler, 1937.* Edward's flirtation with the Nazis, which caused considerable embarrassment to the British government, showed his lack of political acumen

Ward, whom Lady Cynthia Asquith once unfairly dismissed as 'a pretty little fluff', certainly did so. Even though Edward often begged her to marry him, she refused, saying it was clearly out of the question.

The last and greatest love of the king's life did not accept the limits of her position. Born Wallis Warfield in Baltimore in June 1896, her father's death when she was young left her with little more than a name that carried some weight in Maryland. Her mother, whose patrician Virginian ancestors included members of the colonial House of Burgesses, judges, generals, and a governor, had to open their large house to lodgers, and as soon as she could Wallis married Lieutenant Earl Winfield Spencer, an officer in the United States Naval Air Service. Handsome, flamboyant, moody, Earl was a jealous sadist. Within three years they separated. After a passionate affair with a Latin American diplomat in Washington, Wallis escaped quite literally on a slow boat to China, where in Shanghai she enjoyed a 'delightful friendship' with a young Englishman, Robbie, and in Peking began a lifelong relationship with Herman Rogers, whose family estate, Crumwold Hall, was next to Franklin Roosevelt's Hyde Park on the Hudson River. In 1928 this woman of the world came to London, where in July she married Ernest Simpson, who had been born of an American mother and an English father, educated at Harvard, and had served in the Coldstream Guards, becoming a British citizen.

Although Edward had in fact first met Wallis in San Diego in 1920 when she and Lieutenant Spencer were presented to him with scores of other officers and their ladies, he first remembered meeting her at a house party at Melton Mowbray eleven years later. Introduced to Wallis and her husband, he made the usual small talk about the lack of central heating in English houses.

'I am sorry, sir,' she answered with a mocking smile, 'but you have disappointed me.'

'In what way?'

'Every American woman who comes to your country is always asked that same question. I had hoped for something more original from the Prince of Wales.'[33]

Edward was instantly attracted by her honesty and frankness. She had an American openness which contrasted with his father's restraint, and with which he had fallen in love during his visits to the United States. But Wallis's Americanness was both her strength and her fatal flaw. As Sir Samuel Hoare, the First Lord of the

Admiralty, noted after meeting her at a dinner party in July 1936, she was 'very attractive and intelligent, very American and with little or no knowledge of English life'.[34] With her Virginian roots she may well have swallowed whole Thomas Jefferson's exaggerated notions about the prerogatives of an English king, unaware that a constitutional monarch, and head of the Church of England, could never declare his independence from the advice of his ministers and the Archbishop of Canterbury. Ignorant of British history, she did not understand that being the king's mistress was a long-established and honourable profession. Like some Hollywood star, fresh once again from the divorce courts, she insisted on marriage. Risking all, she lost everything in a game she never really comprehended. In December 1936, as her ambitions to become queen, or even the king's morganatic wife, came crashing down, she exclaimed, 'I had no idea that it would be anything like this!'[35]

If Mrs Simpson miscalculated, Edward's abdication was in many respects a deliberate, logical act. By marrying for love and not, as his father and mother incessantly urged, choosing some sensible girl as had his brother George, Edward spurned the sort of arranged marriage that had produced him. By giving up the throne he rejected his father's concepts of honour and duty, putting into effect the threat that he made many years earlier to Mrs Dudley Ward. 'I'm fed up! I've taken all I can stand!' he raged after some particularly painful scene with his father. 'I want no more of this princing! I want to be an ordinary person! I *must* have a life of my own!'

By repudiating the throne, Edward was not only punishing his father, something he never dared to do whilst George V was still alive, but himself too. 'I could have dominated him if I had wanted to. I could have done *anything* with him!' Mrs Dudley Ward recalled. 'He made himself the slave of whomever he loved, and became totally dependent on her. It was his nature: he was a masochist. He *liked* being humbled, degraded. He *begged* for it!'[36] During his life with Wallis, Edward constantly acted like a little boy desperately trying to please his mother. He would go shopping with her, carrying her packages home. He insisted that the duchess receive all the honours he believed due to the wife of an English king, and was bitterly hurt when George VI denied her the title of Royal Highness. He was always doing little things for her: fetching books, her sunglasses, arranging the furniture, lighting her cigarettes, letting her buy whatever she wanted or live where she wished. Sometimes it seemed as if pleasing his wife was the only thing that filled the emptiness of the ex-king's life. Eventually she tired of his cloying attentions. During the 1950s she had a very public liaison with Jimmie Donahue, a homosexual New York playboy and heir to the Woolworth fortune. They were seen dancing and dining together blissfully aware only of each other as the duke looked glumly on. After one especially flagrant episode, Edward was heard to say, 'Darling, are you going to send me to bed in tears again tonight?'[37]

It was the plaintive cry of the battered three-year-old to his implacable yet perversely loving nurse, who spoiled him and then reduced him to tears before presenting him to his mother. At the same time it was the logical response of the charmingly empty man, who after rejecting his patrimony discovered in Wallis Simpson all that had been denied him during his childhood and adolescence. 'I have found her to be utterly without fault, the perfect woman,' Edward told a friend as he lay dying in 1972. 'The Duchess gave me everything that I lacked from my family.'[38]

X

ICH DIEN

No man came to the English throne more reluctantly than George VI. Painfully shy, ill prepared, tormented by a stammer, the prospect of becoming king petrified him. 'Dickie, this is absolutely terrible,' George said to his cousin, Lord Louis Mountbatten, as they watched the Duke of Windsor pack his bags at Fort Belvedere. 'I never wanted this to happen. I'm quite unprepared for it, I'm only a naval officer.'

'George, you're wrong,' Mountbatten replied. 'There is no more fitting preparation for a king than to have been trained in the Navy.'[1]

The abdication was a tremendous blow for the royal family: it was a painful object lesson in how *not* to be a modern constitutional monarch. It showed the fickleness of popular support for the crown. In December 1936 the public took less than ten days to turn Prince Charming into a pumpkin, and make his younger brother a reluctant Cinderella. Instinctively George VI realized that Mountbatten was right. He turned to his training as a naval officer, to his sense of duty, and slowly and painfully managed to restore the crown's prestige. Thirteen years later his heiress, Princess Elizabeth, showed that she had learned the same lesson well. 'I declare before you that my life, whether it be long or short,' she told her future subjects in her twenty-first-birthday broadcast in 1947, 'shall be devoted to your service.'[2] And so today's monarchy has found its *raison d'être* in the motto each of its male heirs bears. '*Ich dien*,' promises every Prince of Wales, 'I serve.'

An extremely happy marriage served George VI well during the abdication crisis. In courting his wife he had displayed that quiet determination that was to help make him an effective king. When he first proposed to Lady Elizabeth Bowes-Lyon, the Earl of Strathmore's youngest daughter, she turned him down, not wanting to lose the opportunity of living a normal life that marriage to the sovereign's younger brother would surely deny her. But two years of gentle persistence eventually won her over. 'I dare say she was very much afraid of the position, but she just found she could not do without him' was the judgment of one of Lady Elizabeth's friends. She and George were married on 23 April 1923. Choosing St George's Day may have been a felicitous omen for an extraordinarily happy marriage. Three years later on 21 April they had their first child. 'You don't know what a tremendous joy it is to Elizabeth and me to have a little girl,' George wrote to his father. 'We always wanted a child to make our happiness complete.'[3]

If there is a theme for Elizabeth II's childhood it is happiness. Her parents enjoyed each other's company and that of their children with an openness rare amongst their peers. As George told his daughter just after she had got married, his wife was 'the most wonderful person in the world'.[4] Elizabeth and her sister Margaret, her junior by four years, grew up in a stable, close, and united family. Their nanny, Mrs Clara Knight – known as 'Allah' since Elizabeth could not pronounce her Christian name – was an old Bowes-Lyon family retainer. They lived at 145 Piccadilly, London, and at Royal Lodge, Windsor, where Elizabeth and Margaret played in Y Bwthyn Bach, a miniature house built in the garden as a present from the Welsh prople. Toys were found all over their parents' houses, for the children were not confined to their nursery, occasionally seen and never heard. Every morning shrieks of laughter could be heard coming from their parents' bedrooms. 'We lived in an ivory tower removed from the real world,' recalled their governess, Marion Crawford; 'then the season was always sunny spring.'[5] When the children's mother engaged Miss Crawford (whom Princess Elizabeth promptly christened 'Crawfie'), she told the new governess, 'We want our children to have a happy childhood which they can always look back on.' The Duke and Duchess of York succeeded beyond their expectations. 'I don't know how they do it,' remarked George as he watched his two girls having a grand time learning how to swim, 'we were always terribly shy and self-conscious.'[6]

One reason why George's childhood had been so traumatic and Elizabeth and Margaret's was one of 'sunny spring' was that the duke expected very little from his children, while his father had demanded much – far too much – from his. 'To spend as long as possible in the open air, to enjoy to the full the pleasures of the country, to be able to dance and draw and appreciate music, to acquire good manners and perfect deportment, and to cultivate all the distinctively feminine graces' were the goals for the daughters' education, the duchess told Crawfie.[7] The governess did not work the girls very hard. Elizabeth and Margaret spent only an hour and a half a day in lessons, reading such untaxing works as *Peter Pan*, and the *Children's Newspaper*, a worthy, but utterly tedious compendium intended for the improvement of the offspring of the middle classes. When pushed beyond this placid regime Elizabeth could misbehave. Sick of being made to write out long lists of verbs she once poured a silver inkwell over Mme Wirz, her French tutor. She much preferred the lessons in constitutional history that she received from Sir Henry Martin, Vice Provost of Eton, a beguiling old eccentric who used to chew sugar lumps concealed in a handkerchief during tutorials. Her father introduced her to contemporary politics by getting her to read *Punch*, and specially marked items from *The Times*. In all it seemed a superb childhood and education for a young lady of high birth, and little hope of doing more in the world than marrying as well as her mother had.

The abdication changed everything.

Understandably the Duke and Duchess of York tried to shield their children from the scandal. The duchess, like Queen Mary, the Queen Mother, hated Mrs Simpson, with a passion that lasted half a century, for what she did to the crown and royal family. 'We must take what is coming to us and make the best of it', was the duchess's sensible Scottish comment on learning that she was to become queen. Elizabeth found Edward VIII's behaviour, the government's reaction, and her parents' metamorphosis all very hard to understand, explaining to her even more confused younger sister, 'I think Uncle David wants to marry Mrs Baldwin, and Mr Baldwin does not like it.'[8] Even more difficult was the role thrust upon her afterwards. Whilst the Duke of Windsor hobnobbed with Nazis or lounged in the sun, George VI publicized his daughters in order to stress the virtues of his own stable family life in contrast to his brother's wanderings. He gave them prominent roles in the Coronation, put their profiles on stamps, and in all stimulated so much worldwide interest that Elizabeth appeared on the cover of *Time* magazine.

Her growing public prominence exacerbated relations with her sister. As it became obvious that her parents would not have a son, Elizabeth's importance increased as that of Margaret (who may have felt that they were disappointed because she was not a boy), waned – some say so painfully that she has never fully recovered. Elizabeth realized this transformation but slowly. After her confirmation at the age of fifteen she vowed, 'I will try to be good, won't I,

62 *Princess Elizabeth aged two, with her mother, the Duchess of York.* Elizabeth had a secure childhood in a close family, and, until her uncle's abdication, no expectations of greatness

Crawfie?'⁹ Her reaction was very similar to that of Queen Victoria.

Elizabeth was confirmed during the Second World War, a particularly trying time to go through the difficult phase of adolescence. When war broke out in September 1939 the royal family were in Scotland, where the children remained on their parents' return to London. They were reunited at Sandringham for Christmas, and then spent the rest of the war at Windsor. Most of the time Crawfie looked after the two girls whilst the king and queen commuted to London, or toured factories, depots and dockyards to encourage the war effort. The girls tried to do their bit. They collected saucepans to turn into Spitfires, dug vegetable gardens, and followed the progress of the war avidly. The sinking of HMS *Royal Oak* at Scapa Flow in 1939 was a particular blow. 'Crawfie, it can't be! All those nice sailors,' exclaimed Elizabeth.¹⁰ Like many English families the Windsors would listen to Lord Haw Haw's propaganda with fascinated revulsion, pelting the radio with books and cushions whenever he became especially nauseous. Like most children growing up during the war, food became a major preoccupation for Elizabeth and Margaret. They would save their weekly egg (a treat so precious that spies were actually given two before being parachuted into enemy territory) for Sunday mornings, and longed for sweets (of which American servicemen seemed to be an inexhaustible supply).

The main relief from wartime life at Windsor were the Christmas pantomimes that the princesses put on: silly, hackneyed, full of the most wonderfully awful puns, they were the perfect escape for the royal family and their friends. Many of the audience were young officers from the battalion of Grenadiers stationed at Windsor to protect the royal family from German paratroopers. The girls would invite the subalterns to teas, over which Elizabeth presided with surprising maturity, and were saddened whenever they learned that one of the young guardsmen had been killed in battle.

On becoming eighteen Elizabeth registered for National Service, as required by law. Normally a dutiful daughter, she rebelled against her father's ruling that being a privy councillor and staying at home with him was service enough to the nation. Eventually he allowed her to join the Auxiliary Training Service as a second subaltern. As an officer she learned how to drive, look after soldiers, and service cars. The army taught her another, more important lesson. 'You've no idea what a business it has been,' the future sovereign wrote to Crawfie about a forthcoming visit to her unit by her aunt Princess Mary. 'Everyone working so hard – spit and polishing the whole day long. Now I realize what must happen when Papa and Mama go anywhere. That's something I shall never forget.'[11]

Something else neither of the king's daughters ever forgot was the end of the war. The celebrations at Germany's surrender were uninhibited. Crowds surged around Buckingham Palace cheering the royal family and Winston Churchill as they waved back from the balcony. Afterwards the king let his children leave the palace to join the festivities. With a few young officers they roamed the streets, now lit for the first time after five and a half years of blackout, forming congas with passers-by (only one of whom, a Dutch serviceman, recognized them), as they milled up and down the Mall chanting, 'We want the king!' Princess Margaret remembered, 'I never had such a beautiful evening.'[12] George VI agreed, writing in his diary that night, 'Poor Darlings, they never had much fun yet.'[13]

Elizabeth idolized her father. According to Group Captain Peter Townsend, who served as George VI's equerry and knew him and his family very well, 'Princess Elizabeth was the King's pride, she was his heir, his understudy, his affectionate admirer, and played her role, as he did his, dutifully, punctiliously, and charmingly.'[14] The admiration of father and daughter was mutual. She admired his sense of duty and determination, particularly in overcoming his stutter. She enjoyed the sense of fun this immensely shy man was able to create within his immediate family. But unlike her sister Elizabeth was unable to still the darker depths of the king's personality, those sudden, intense rages that his family called his 'gnashes', that were spawned like tornadoes from the trauma of his earliest years. 'Princess Margaret was the king's joy,' Townsend recalled. 'She amused . . . delighted . . . enchanted him.'

George VI and Elizabeth had one major disagreement. Quite simply the king could not believe that his daughter had fallen in love with virtually the first eligible man she had met.

The first time Elizabeth and Philip were conscious of each other's existence was in July 1939, when George VI took his family to visit his old school, the Royal Naval College, Dartmouth. Stories about the visit vary. Some say that Philip, an eighteen-year-old cadet, was irritated at having to entertain his two female cousins, although the next day he did row after the departing royal yacht long after the rest of the farewell florilla of small boats had turned home. 'The young fool' was George VI's comment at the time, although the king's official biographer afterwards asserted that it was at Dartmouth that Elizabeth first fell in love with the man whom she was

63 *Conversation Piece at Royal Lodge, Windsor*, 1950, by Sir James Gunn. This painting of the royal family taking tea at Windsor became extremely popular. The portrayal of a family obviously enjoying each other's company, with the daughters respectfully listening to their father, must have reassured an older generation disturbed by the upheavals of post-war England

64 *George VI initiates his daughter into the paperwork of monarchy, 1942.* Edward VIII's abdication was a shattering blow for his brother, plunging the diffident new king (who stuttered badly) into the centre of public life. George VI carefully instructed his eldest daughter in the paperwork which is one of the most important and onerous duties of a democratic monarch, and for which he himself was unprepared. She proved an apt pupil: Harold Wilson said admiringly of Queen Elizabeth, 'She certainly does her homework'

to marry eight years later. We do know that at Christmas 1939 she pestered her father to send a card to Midshipman The Prince Philip, doing convoy duty aboard HMS *Ramillies*. Even though 'Chips' Channon as early as 1941 reported the rumour that 'He is to be our Prince Consort,' and for much of the war Elizabeth kept Philip's photograph in her room, the king discouraged any thought of marriage. 'We both think she is too young for that now, as she has never met any young men of her own age,' he wrote to the King of Greece when he first formally raised the match in 1944. 'I like Philip. He is intelligent, has a good sense of humour and thinks on things in the right way. . . .'[15]

Obstacle after obstacle impeded the marriage. First the war had to be won, then the question of Philip's nationality, which was further complicated by the Greek civil war, had to be settled, and finally Elizabeth had to accompany her parents on a tour of South Africa, before George VI would allow them to announce their engagement on 10 July 1947.

Shortly before the marriage on 20 November, Elizabeth told her mother that the long wait 'was all for the best'. A few days after the wedding, her father, guilty about the delay, wrote, 'I was so proud of you and thrilled at having you so close to me on our long walk in Westminster Abbey, but when I handed you to the Archbishop I felt I had lost something so precious.'[16] Few fathers could have put it better – that mixture of sadness, pride, and joy. The satisfaction of one generation sure that it had done its duty – and done its duty rather well, combined with the regret that his close-knit family could never be quite the same. Yet the king could take pleasure in the fact that his daughter had married a naval officer – as he had been – and presented him with a grandson, Charles, in 1948, and granddaughter, Anne, two years later. When Elizabeth and Philip went off on official tours the children came to stay with their grandparents. During the ten months Philip commanded his own ship, HMS *Magpie*, Elizabeth was able to live a life as close to that of a normal naval officer's wife as the heir to the throne can expect. Thus the king's sudden death early on the morning of 6 February 1952 came as a terrible blow, for it not only deprived her of a beloved father, but also of any further chance of living as a wife and mother without the distractions of being queen.

It is, of course, far too soon to say with any confidence what effect Elizabeth's childhood has had on her as queen. For one thing her reign is far from over. If she lives, as have most of her female

ancestors, into her eighties she will be queen well in the twenty-first
century. Detailed and reliable formation about the intimate life of
the royal family is hard to obtain – unlike tabloid speculation, which
may be gained from any newsagent's practically every morning for
a few pence. The royal family live in a cocoon of privacy made even
more inpenetrable by excessive publicity. None the less, it cannot
be denied that there have been few modern monarchs as successful
and popular as Elizabeth II. She had an extraordinarily happy childhood, untroubled by any great expectations, and overcame the
difficulties of her sudden elevation and a wartime adolescence. She
had a warm and satisfying relationship with her father – tinged with
just enough rebellion and she married well.

Philip was born on 10 June 1921 on the dining room table of
'Mon Repos', once the residence of the British Consul General in
Corfu. His mother was Alice of Battenburg, his father Prince
Andrew of Greece, who was court-martialled after the Turks routed
his army corps in Anatolia in 1922. The Greek government might
well have shot him had not the Admiralty, at George V's insistence,
sent HMS *Calypso* to rescue the prince, and pick up his family from
Corfu. So precipitate was their flight that Philip had to spend his
first night aboard the British cruiser in a cot the sailors knocked up
from orange boxes.

Exile destroyed his parents' marriage. Prince Andrew found his
way to Monte Carlo, where he became an embittered small-time
playboy. Princess Alice wandered around Europe, spending the war
in Athens, where she hid refugees from the Germans. In 1947 she
founded the Christian Sisterhood of Martha and Mary, wearing the
robe of the order until she died in 1969. So Philip's childhood was
rather unsettled. He stayed with relatives in France, Germany, and
England, and attended a day school in Paris before going to Cheam
preparatory school in Hampshire. 'We weren't well off,' he recalled,
although his mother was not, as was rumoured, reduced to running
a gift shop in Paris to make ends meet. At the age of twelve Philip
was sent to Salem School in Germany, which Kurt Hahn had just
founded. Since Hahn was Jewish the Nazis took over the school the
following year, forcing Philip to transfer to Gordonstoun, the branch
just opened in Scotland. At Gordonstoun Philip shone. A keen
sportsman and a good leader, his intellectual faculties were not as
strained as they might have been by a more traditional public school.
He became guardian, or head boy, and left for the Royal Naval
College, Dartmouth, with glowing references from Hahn. He did

well at Dartmouth, and served with distinction during the Second World War. For most of the first two decades after his parents' exile Philip was a man without much of a family or home. 'I once or twice spent Christmas as Windsor because I had nowhere particular to go,' he recalled of his wartime leaves, adding with that self-deprecating humour that often hides real hurt, 'They're always glad to see you. The cooking's all right.'[17]

As soon as he could Philip brought a breath of fresh air into the royal family. His first son, Prince Charles, was born on 14 November 1948 without a senior minister of the crown in attendance, breaking a precedent that went back at least to the 'warming pan baby' rumours of the seventeenth century. 'Don't you think he is adorable?' enthused Elizabeth. 'Anyway this particular boy's new parents could not be more proud of him.'[18]

As Charles grew up they became worried about his development. At best Charles was a plodder, a homebody, who much preferred watching television to reading books. Indeed, at the age of five he could not read, and his mother thought him too immature to take lessons with other children. So she hired Catherine Peebles, a kind but firm Scot untainted by any formal training in education, to act as his governess and teach him French, geography, history, religion and mathematics.

When Philip decided three years later that his son should attend Hill House, a preparatory school close to Buckingham Palace, he was not only breaking with tradition, but taking a considerable academic risk. In addition the young boy had to cope with the hordes of reporters and photographers who camped outside the school, dogging each one of the new pupil's steps. Eventually the Queen asked the editors to remove their people, and let Charles settle down to spend two fairly happy terms at Hill House.

In September 1957 Charles entered his father's old school, Cheam. 'He dreaded going to school,' recalled his nurse, Mabel Anderson. Charles remembered his first months there as the most miserable of his life. 'You won't be able to jump up and down on *these* beds,' his mother told him as they were being shown around the spartan dormitories. Gradually things improved. After they had published stories on sixty-eight of the eighty-eight days of Charles's first term, the Queen invited the Fleet Street editors to lunch, and warned them that they were jeopardizing an important experiment in royal education. They agreed to call off the publicity, allowing Charles to take part in amateur dramatics, singing and playing rugby. 'They always put me in the second row,' he remembered, 'the worst place in the scrum.'[19]

At Cheam Charles came to terms with his future. 'I don't think it is something that dawns on you with the most ghastly inexorable sense,' he told a radio interviewer years later about the realization that someday he would become king. 'I didn't wake up in my pram and say Yippee. . . . But I think it just dawns on you, you know, slowly. . . .'[20] The day it dawned most dramatically on the heir to the throne may well have been 26 July 1958. Charles and a group of friends were watching the Queen close the Commonwealth Games at Cardiff on television in Peter Beck's study at Cheam. When she announced that she was making her eldest son Prince of Wales, and would in due time invest him at Caernarvon Castle, Beck, Cheam's headmaster, noted a look of acute embarrassment flash across the surprised nine-year-old's face. 'It was then that he fully realized the loneliness of his position,' Beck recalled, 'and the awful fate that lay in store for him.'[21]

At about the same time Charles's father determined that he should go to Gordonstoun. Apart from the fact that it was hundreds of miles from Fleet Street (unlike Eton), Gordonstoun was like Cheam, his father's old school. Having enjoyed his time there, Philip assumed that his very different son would do the same. He was wrong. Charles's first few years at Gordonstoun were particularly difficult. Initially other boys tended to shy away from the prince; social climbers pushed themselves forward, the decent sort held back. An intensely reserved child, Charles found it hard to rebuff the former and encourage the latter. As often as possible he would escape to Balmoral, where he would beg the Queen Mother to ask his parents to remove him from Gordonstoun.

With its emphasis on physical activities such as sailing and mountain climbing, Gordonstoun was not the best place for a gentle, introverted boy such as Charles. Certainly the intrusions of the press made life well nigh unbearable. The 'cherry brandy' incident hurt him deeply. In June 1963 Charles was in Stornoway, having just landed from the school's yacht *Pinta*. A crowd gathered. He took refuge in the Crown Hotel. Finding himself in the bar he was asked if he would like a drink, and without thinking ordered a cherry brandy. A passing journalist reported the scoop, which quickly turned into a press sensation that implied that the fourteen-year-old's attempt to break Scotland's licensing laws was a dire threat to the future of the monarchy, if not to that of Western civilization as

65 *The Queen playing with Prince Charles and Princess Anne at Balmoral, 1952*. This charmingly spontaneous photograph could be of almost any young family

66 *Prince Charles walking with other pupils while at his first school, Hill House.* Charles. was the first English heir apparent to be educated with other children at school

Fleet Street knew it. As a result Charles was demoted at school and lost privileges. His bitterness towards the press increased the following year when a journalist stole and published one of his exercise books. More wounding than the appearance of his essays, rather prosaic pieces on the constitution, was the unfounded allegation that he had sold his autograph because his parents were mean in sending him pocket money.

Charles's school days improved greatly in January 1966 when he flew to Australia to attend Timbertop, an extension of Geelong Grammar School, some two hundred miles north of Melbourne. For one thing his equerry, Squadron Leader David Checketts, handled the press competently, letting them follow the prince around on his first day at school taking all the pictures they wanted. Charles enjoyed the camaraderie of the outback, soon winning the ultimate Australian accolade, 'Pommie bastard'. He worked hard on his A-levels, enjoyed supervising the younger boys, and had his interest in anthropology awakened by a trip to Papua and New Guinea. On leaving Australia to fly back to Gordonstoun he described his six-month stay as 'the most wonderful period of my life'. David Checketts described the change: 'I went there with a boy, and returned with a man.'[22] This was readily apparent during Charles's final year at Gordonstoun. He was elected head of his house, and then head of school; his work improved enough to pass A-levels in History and French.

Nearly two years earlier the Queen had invited a number of experts, including the Archbishop of Canterbury, the prime minister, amd the chairman of the Committee of University Vice Chancellors, to discuss the heir's future. Late into the night, and after much talk, Lord Mountbatten's suggestion prevailed: Charles should go to Cambridge, attend Sandhurst, Dartmouth and Cranwell, and then spend several years in the armed forces.

The Queen chose Trinity College: its dons were amongst the best at Cambridge; its master, Lord Butler, was a distinguished statesmen and old family friend; her father had spent a year at Trinity, three-quarters of whose undergraduates were from state schools. On arriving at the university Charles tended to befriend public school men. He quickly won a half blue at polo, and took part in student dramatics, where he displayed a talent for mimicry and 'Goon Show' type humour. At Cambridge Charles lived a normal life, shopping in the market, studying at the Seeley, and attending lectures with so little fuss that graduate students taking seminars in the room next door never noticed. In his first year Charles read Anthropology, and according to Lord Butler, might well have taken a First had he not switched to History for his second and final years. Charles eventually obtained a Lower Second, a highly creditable degree in view of the many extracurricular demands on his time. He had to attend state funerals and the opening of parliament. During the spring of his final year he spent six weeks at University College, Aberystwyth, studying Welsh, an extraordinary difficult tongue, to prepare for his investiture as Prince of Wales.

The investiture was a great success. Charles spoke Welsh fluently, playing his part in the mock medieval ceremony without embarrassment, and to the obvious satisfaction of the millions who watched on television.

In many ways Charles's investite and graduation in 1969 marked his coming of age. He spent the next half-dozen years in the services, eventually commanding a minesweeper, before becoming his mother's understudy, and trying (without much luck) to act as a highly placed social worker. Not until his marriage to Lady Diana Spencer on 29 July 1981 was he to enjoy the popularity he had known a dozen years earlier at Caernarvon. The public rejoicing was utterly sincere, being a blend of that joy which attends all weddings, with their promise of hope and transparent happiness, mixed with widespread relief that the Prince of Wales had become a mature adult who had won a beautiful yet sensible young woman.

Of the several people who played a part in this transformation Prince Philip was the most important. 'My father had a particularly strong influence, and it was very good for me,' Charles admitted. 'I had perfect confidence in his judgment.'23 It was Philip who insisted that his sons attend his old schools, for he wanted them to grow up with children of their own age, learning the self-discipline of community living. While in public Prince Philip always appears as the deferential consort, walking slightly bowed, hands behind his back, two paces after the sovereign, in private he is the head of his family. A traditional paternalist, he tried to spend as much time as he could with his children, perhaps to make up for the neglect of his own youth. He attempted to interest them in his favourite sports and hobbies (failing with Charles, who disliked sailing and water-colour painting), because he believed that once a child gained confidence in one activity, it would spill over to the rest. Philip insisted that his children make their own beds, do household chores, and that the nursery servants call them by their first names. His wife

67 *The royal family gathered for the Silver Wedding anniversary of the Queen and the Duke of Edinburgh, 1972* (photograph by Patrick Lichfield). Today much of the royal family's popularity depends on the careful manipulation of the media. In this photograph twenty members of the extended royal family are gathered for an occasion familiar to us all; and yet, as the grand paintings on the wall show, this is no ordinary clan. The popularity of family sagas on television suggests that people like to follow the lives of fictional families which they can identify with, but never emulate. The royal family is the real-life equivalent

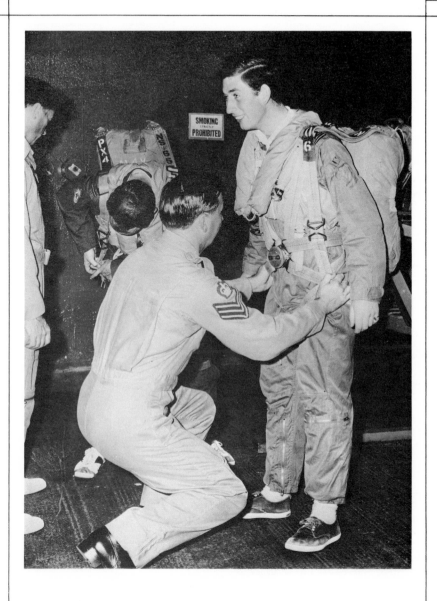

68 *Prince Charles about to take his first parachute jump.* People expect royalty to be interested in and enjoy every public duty. Charles gives the impression of doing so, by continuing to smile even as he is about to leap into space. His years at his father's old school, Gordonstoun, helped him become an 'action man' who flew planes, underwent commando training and commanded a naval ship agreed. Once when Charles lost a dog's lead on the palace grounds she sent the young boy back to find it with the admonition 'Leads cost money.' Responsibility and honesty were the family's cardinal virtues: telling a lie its most heinous crime.

While Philip is in many ways an authoritarian character (who once told General Stroessner, the fascist dictator of Paraguay, 'It's a pleasant change to be in a country that isn't ruled by its people'), he could be surprisingly democratic with his children.[24] As they grew older, he would set out options rather than giving them a direct order. He recognized that children go through great changes, sometimes growing up with pleasant ease, and at others becoming cross-grained with maddening stubbornness. He believed that his children must observe him and the Queen. 'I learned the way a monkey learns,' Charles recalled, 'by watching its parents.'[25]

As he grew older, a more objective judgment replaced Charles's hero worship of his father. He became more intimate with his grand-uncle, Lord Mountbatten. Mountbatten was one of those truly heroic figures in the history of the British royal family. A friend of Edward VIII, a courageous destroyer captain, Director of Combined Operations and a Supreme Allied Commander in the Second World War, he had a profound influence on Charles. The two used to see each other at least once a month, sharing secrets that Charles could never possibly confide to his parents. Mountbatten's murder by Irish terrorists in 1979 hurt the Prince of Wales, like the rest of the royal family, deeply. Charles signed his wreath to his honorary grandfather as from his 'honorary grandson'.

Charles's real grandmother, Queen Elizabeth, the Queen Mother, had helped him through the difficult first years at Gordonstoun, which he might well at times have held against his father. Perhaps this is why he moved closer to his mother as he grew older. After all she was the person best able to train him to be sovereign. Like all families, that of Windsor has had its tensions. Charles, for instance, has been more tolerant of his Aunt Margaret's foibles than his father, while having little time for his brother-in-law.

In all the influence of school, parents, grandmother, grand-uncle, as well as the relatively recent effects of marriage and fatherhood, have produced an able young man, fully aware of the precarious nature of his inheritance. Charles does not need a second-class honours degree in History from Cambridge to know that the twentieth century has not been kind to monarchs. During his grandfather's reign alone, five emperors, eight kings, and eighteen minor dynasties lost power. In contrast the House of Windsor has been extraordinarily good at surviving – it even changed its name from Saxe-Coburg-Gotha to help it do so during the First World War. Notwithstanding the magic, sentimentality, and occasional nonsense that surrounds the royal family, it has taken a hard, cold approach in adapting a medieval institution to this century. Even though Prince Philip once told a Canadian audience, 'If the people don't want it, then they won't have it,' he and his family have effectively persuaded them that royalty is what they really wanted all along.[26]

The problems of doing so are immense. Monarchs selected by the random chance of birth contradict the fundamental principles of egalitarian democracy. Preference given to male over female heirs offends sexual equality. Palaces, royal yachts, the Queen's Flight – all the blatant signs of conspicuous consumption – often seem in poor taste in a kingdom of declining resources and expectations. When Victoria was Empress of India, the monarchy was the symbol of a white-dominated Empire, as well as the head of the Church of England. Since then it has tried to become the centre of a multi-national and multi-religious Commonwealth, and may well have achieved some success in that goal, until Britain changed direction by forsaking the Commonwealth to join the Common Market – a place where the price of butter stirs far greater passions than the predicament of princes.

Admittedly the readers of Common Market newspapers seem to feel a fascination with England's royalty that is in no way diminished by considerations of credibility. Between 1952 and 1972 the French press alone published sixty-three reports that the Queen would abdicate, seventy-three that she would divorce Philip, and ninety-two that she was pregnant. Relations between the royal family and the English press have been less fantastic, although more painful, mainly because journalists have cloaked professional misconduct and bad taste with pious declarations of loyalty, and apologies so grovelling that they often feel obliged to repeat the offence for the further titillation of their readers and their profits. Admittedly the royal family have brought about many of their own difficulties. Most royal press secretaries believe their function is the prevention of news about the royal family, rather than its management in a mutually acceptable way. An initial denial from the Palace made the 'cherry brandy' incident all the more painful for Charles. In contrast Squadron Leader Checkett's enlightened handling of the Australian press helped turn Charles's time at Timbertop into a pleasant success.

69 *The Prince and Princess of Wales with Prince William and Prince Harry at Kensington Palace, 1984* (Photo: Snowdon). While the British public enjoyed Charles's formative years, they wanted him to settle down, and greeted his marriage to Lady Diana Spencer, an attractive and eminently sensible girl, with considerable relief. The birth of a male heir as soon as proper afterwards was an additional bonus, guaranteeing the future of an important British institution when that of so many others seems in jeopardy

Gradually the royal family has learned to use the media with consummate skill, realizing, as Prince Charles put it, 'If the photographers weren't interested, that would be the time to start worrying.' Television, with its insatiable appetite for the visual action of parades, bands, coaches and crowds, has been especially efficacious, Queen Elizabeth discovered this at the start of her reign when she insisted, over the objections of several ministers, that her coronation be televised. The 1967 television documentary, *The Royal Family*, was a public relations triumph, as have been the televised state occasions such as weddings, the opening of parliament, the Silver Jubilee, and the investiture of the Prince of Wales. After the latter, for instance, only 4 per cent of the Welsh people polled said they wanted a republic.[27]

The royal family both mirrors and matches that of most of its subjects. For instance two of them, of the tens of thousands who waited through the long and very cold night to file past George VI's coffin lying in state in Westminster Hall were overheard saying:

'He's my king, and I want to say goodbye to him, just as I would if he was a member of my family.'

'Yes, that's right. Same as if he were a father, really.'[28]

On the other hand, the royal family, rather like a mafia clan, must be suspicious of outsiders lest they betray confidences. They regarded Marion Crawford's publication of her memoirs in 1950 as a heinous betrayal. Thus the royal family tends to be more of an extended family than most. After all whom can you trust if you can't trust relatives? Second cousins play with each other, the brother-in-law photographs them, the heir to the throne turned to his great-uncle as a mentor in a way that many young men do to their college tutors. Yet the cost of this vast clan has prompted much public comment. At times the British people want it both ways. They would prefer a religious royal family, yet they hardly ever go to church. They want a stable, harmonious family, with all the Victorian trappings of morality, while finding their own way into other people's beds or the divorce courts in ever-increasing numbers. Despite high levels of unemployment, most British subjects believe that every young man should go out and get a good job, and yet they deny Prince Charles the choice of a career. He can, of course, fly RAF jets (preferably with an instructor in the rear seat), he may even be allowed to make parachute jumps (into the sea with plenty of frogmen in attendance), but he could never enter business, the law, or the church. No wonder the heir to the throne has complained, 'There is no set out role for me. It depends entirely on what I make of it . . . I'm really rather an awkward problem.'

Pollsters have confirmed the awkwardness of his position, for public attitudes to the crown are as fickle as they are vocal. While support for the monarchy remains broadly based, the proportion of those favouring a republic averaging only about 12 per cent since the war, it has never been very profound. Edward VIII discovered this in less than ten days. While ultra-royalists responded to Lord Altrincham's attack on the Queen as 'a priggish schoolgirl, captain of the hockey team' by mailing him parcels of excrement, polls showed wide agreement with his criticisms. Thus those who loudly profess to serve the crown best may do it the greatest disservice by shielding it from unpleasant realities.

At the same time polls reveal a bedrock of support for monarchy as an institution, as opposed to the particular individual who happens to sit upon the throne. A 1969 survey revealed, for instance, that the public valued the royal family for four main reasons.[29] First because it provided a basis for political stability. Ministers come and go, but the sovereign is there for decades as a symbol of national unity with no power except to deny it to professional politicians. Second, the monarch is a focus for affections and vicarious fantasies, as shown by the large number of dreams people have concerning the royal family. If, as Malcolm Muggeridge sneered, the House of Windsor has become a 'royal soap opera . . . a sort of substitute or ersatz religion', well, people need escapism.[30] Thirdly, the monarchy sets an example of familial and public service, which becomes even more precious as existing standards seem to erode. If that is public hypocrisy so be it: a changing world cannot live by logic alone. Finally, the royal family provides the pageants and ceremonials that not merely entertain tourists from abroad, but at home provide excitement, and the security that each year the Colour will be trooped, parliament will open, the Guard will change, and there will always be an England.

To try and bring up a child to fulfil all these contradictory and inchoate goals, would, of course, be impossible. It is as hard to predict the future of the royal family as it is our own. As we have seen, the relationships between childhood and adult life are far from ordained. Poor childhoods have produced great monarchs: idyllic adolescences ineffectual kings. Thus the morning of royalty becomes in many ways everyman's dawn. All any of us can do, be we kings or commoners, is our best, and hope that when our day as parents is over we may agree with Prince Philip: 'What a relief it is when you find you've actually brought up a reasonable and civilized human being.'[31]

NOTES

II William I

1 Quoted by Henry Loyn, *The Norman Conquest* (New York, 1967), 34.
2 David C. Douglas, 'William the Conqueror: Duke and King', in C. T. Chevallier (ed.), *The Norman Conquest* (New York, 1966), 51, and *William the Conqueror* (Berkeley and Los Angeles, 1964), 374.
3 William of Jumièges, in David C. Douglas and George W. Greenaway (eds), *English Historical Documents, 1042–1189* (London, 1981), II, 229. Henceforth cited as *EHD*.
4 William of Poitiers, *EHD*, II, 236.
5 *EHD*, II, 235.
6 *EHD*, II, 239.
7 *EHD*, II, 240.
8 *EHD*, II, 248.
9 Chronicle, D, *EHD*, II, 150.
10 *EHD*, II, 306–9.
11 *EHD*, II, 311.
12 Sigmund Freud, *Collected Papers* (London, 1952), IV, 367. For a popular piece on the same topic see David McCullough, 'Sons and Mothers: the making of powerful men', *Psychology Today*, XVII, 3 (March 1983), 32–9.
13 For the significance of a similar 'mistake' see Sigmund Freud, *Leonardo da Vinci and a Memory of His Childhood* (New York, 1964), 69–72.
14 *EHD*, II, 307.
15 Quoted by Maurice Ashley, *The Life and Times of William I* (London, 1973), 94.
16 William of Poitiers, *EHD*, II, 234.
17 Ordericus Vitalis, *The Ecclesiastical History of England and Normandy* (London, 1856), I, 463.
18 Erik H. Erikson, *Insight and Responsibility* (New York, 1964), 202.
19 The thesis that power can be a compensation for childhood deprivation has been advanced by numerous writers, including Fred I. Greenstein, *Personality and Politics* (New York, 1975).
20 *EHD*, II, 306.

III John

1 J.C. Holt, *King John* (London, 1963), 26–7.
2 K. Norgate, *John Lackland* (London, 1902), 286.
3 J.R. Green, quoted by Warren Hollister, 'King John and the Historians', *Journal of British Studies*, I (1962), 2.
4 M. Ashley, *The Life and Times of King John* (London, 1972), 204, calls him 'an extremely maligned monarch'. See also Alan Lloyd, *The Maligned Monarch* (Garden City, NY, 1972).
5 W. Stubbs, *The Historical Works of Gervase of Canterbury* (London, 1880), II, 100, quoted by W.L. Warren, *King John* (London, 1961), 2. Warren's is the best modern biography.
6 Quoted by Norgate, *op. cit.*, 9.
7 J.T. Appleby, *John, King of England* (London, 1960), 40.
8 Warren, *op. cit.*, 90.
9 Quoted by Norgate, *op. cit.*, 10–11.
10 Warren, *op. cit.*, 258–9.
11 Quoted by Marion Meade, *Eleanor of Aquitaine* (New York, 1977), 191.
12 Gervase of Canterbury, quoted by Meade, *op. cit.*, 268.
13 Anonymous monk from Barnwell, Cambs., quoted by Warren, *op. cit.*, 90.
14 That Geoffrey became Bishop of Ely in 1225 would suggest that stories of his horrible death at John's command were unfounded.
15 Quoted by Caroline Bingham, *The Crowned Lions* (Newton Abbot, 1978), 148.
16 W.L. Warren, 'John in Ireland in 1185', in John Bossy and Peter Jupp (eds), *Essays Presented to Michael Roberts* (Belfast, 1976), 11–23.
17 Quoted by Warren, *King John*, 176.

IV Henry VIII

1 F.A. Mumby, *The Youth of Henry VIII* (Boston, 1913), 127; N.S. Tjernegel, *Henry VIII and the Lutherans* (St Louis, 1965), 19.
2 A.S. McNalty, *Henry VIII: A Difficult Patient* (London, 1952), 18–23. Ove Brinch, 'The Medical Problems of Henry VIII', *Centaurus*, V, 3–4 (1958), 339–69.
3 Mumby, *op. cit.*, 5. *The Epistles of Erasmus*, ed. F.M. Nichols (New York, 1962), II, 201.
4 M. St Clare Byrne (ed.), *The Letters of King Henry VIII* (New York, 1968), 4.
5 Mumby, *op. cit.*, 61.
6 *Ibid.*, 49.
7 *Ibid.*, 129.
8 J. Gairdner and R.H. Brodie (eds), *Letters and Papers, Foreign and Domestic, of the Reign of Henry VIII* (London, 1862–1910), II, 395.
9 Mumby, *op. cit.*, 129.

10 Gairdner and Brodie, *op. cit.*, III, 2555.
11 Mumby, *op. cit.*, 98.
12 Gairdner and Brodie, *op. cit.*, XIII, ii, 804.
13 Byrne, *op. cit.*, 62.
14 Gairdner and Brodie, *op. cit.*, IV, 3802 and 6290.
15 William Roper, *Life of More*, quoted by J. J. Scarisbrick, *Henry VIII* (London, 1968), 16–17; this is the standard biography.
16 Mumby, *op. cit.*, 131.
17 Byrne, *op. cit.*, 128.
18 J.C. Flugel, 'The Character and Married Life of Henry VIII', in Bruce Mazlish (ed.), *Psychoanalysis and History* (Englewood Cliffs, NJ, 1963), 124–49.
19 Leviticus 20:21. Deuteronomy 25:5, however, commands that 'when brethren dwell together, and one of them dieth without children, the wife of the deceased shall not marry to another; but his brother shall take her, and raise up seed for his brother.
20 Lacey Baldwin Smith, *Henry VIII: The Mask of Royalty* (Boston, 1971). Miles Shore, 'Henry VIII and the Crisis of Generativity', *Journal of Interdisciplinary History*, 2 (1972), 359–90.
21 Gairdner and Brodie, *op. cit.*, IV, dcxvi.

V   Elizabeth I

1 Joseph M. Levine, *Elizabeth* (Englewood Cliffs, NJ, 1969), 12.
2 Sir Henry Ellis, *Original Letters Illustrative of English History* (London, 1846), II, 78–83.
3 G. B. Harrison, *The Letters of Queen Elizabeth I* (New York, 1968), 4–5.
4 M.A.E. Green, *Letters of Royal and Illustrious Ladies* (London, 1846), III, 193–4.
5 Harrison, *op. cit.*, 7–8.
6 *Ibid.*, 8.
7 F.A. Mumby, *The Girlhood of Queen Elizabeth: a narrative from contemporary letters* (London, 1909), 41.
8 Harrison, *op. cit.*, 11–12.
9 Mumby, *op. cit.*, 51.
10 Harrision, *op. cit.*, 19–21.
11 John Foxe, *Actes and Monuments*, ed. Josiah Pratt (London, 1870), VIII, 609.
12 *State Papers relating to the custody of Princess Elizabeth at Woodstock* (Norfolk Archaeological Society, IV, 1855), 150–7.
13 *Ibid.*, 223–4.
14 Foxe, *op. cit.*, VIII, 619.
15 *Ibid.*, 624.
16 J. Strype, *The Life of the Learned Sir T. Smith* (Oxford, 1820), 249–50.
17 'The Distresses of the Commonwealth, and the means to remedy them', in *Calendar of State Papers, Domestic, 1547–80* (London, 1856–72), 119ff.

18 Mumby, *op. cit.*, 70.
19 Harrison, *op. cit.*, 15. Simonds D'Ewes, *The Journal of all the parliaments during the reign of Queen Elizabeth* (London, 1682), 660.
20 R. Brown, C. Bentinck and H. Brown (eds), *Calendar of State Papers, Venetian* (London, 1864–98), VI, 1058–60.
21 Mumby, *op. cit.*, 64.
22 Sir Arthur S. MacNalty, *Elizabeth Tudor: The Lonely Queen* (New York, 1961), 101.
23 J. Bruce, *Letters of Queen Elizabeth and King James VI* (Camden Society, 1849), 167.
24 Sir John Harrington, *Nugae Antiquae*, ed. Thomas Park (London, 1804), 320.
25 MacNalty, *op. cit.*, 60.
26 Levine, *op. cit.*, 144.
27 Green, *op. cit.*, III, 193–4.
28 Harrison, *op. cit.*, 103.
29 Sir John Neale, *Queen Elizabeth I* (Garden City, NY, 1957), 61.
30 Sir John Neale, *Elizabeth I and Her Parliaments* (New York, 1966), II, 117.
31 *Ibid.*, 118.

VI   Charles I

1 William Laud, *Works*, ed. W. Scot and J. Bliss (Oxford, 1847–60), III, 147. This chapter is based on Charles Carlton, *Charles I, The Personal Monarch* (London, 1983).
2 *Calendar of State Papers . . . Venice, 1623–3*, 592.
3 Robert Carey, *Memoirs* (Oxford, 1975), 25–6, 66–9.
4 William Lilly, *Life and Death of Charles I* (London, 1654).
5 Alex MacDonald, *Letters to King James the Sixth* (Edinburgh, 1835), xxxviii. See also British Library, Harl. MSS, 6986, 151.
6 Thomas Middleton, *Civitatis Amor* (London, 1616).
7 John Chamberlain, *Letters* (Philadelphia, 1939), II, 32.
8 M.A.E. Green, *Elizabeth of Bohemia* (London, 1849–55), 303.
9 Chamberlain, *Letters*, II, 219. *Calendar of State Papers, Domestic, 1619–23*, 4.
10 Richard Perrinchief, *The Royal Martyr* (London, 1676), 61.
11 G. Goodman, *The Court of King James the First* (London, 1839), 209–10.
12 Sir Charles Petrie, *The Letters, Speeches and Proclamations of King Charles I* (London, 1968), 272.
13 George Chalmer, *The Poetic Remains of the Scottish Kings* (London, 1827), 203.
14 Anthony Weldon, 'The Court and Character of King James', in W. Scot (ed.), *The Secret History of King James I* (London, 1811), I, 443.
15 British Library, Add. MSS 4176, 71.

16 Sir Francis Bacon, *Works* (1858), 55. Historical Manuscripts Commission, *Bath*, II, 68.
17 James Howell, *Epistolae-Ho-Elianae*, ed. Joseph Jacobs (London, 1892), I, 164.
18 *Ibid.*, 168–70.
19 Public Record Office, SP 78/72/275.
20 Quoted by Margaret Pickel, *Charles I as a Patron of Poetry and Drama* (London, 1936), 36.

VII   George III

1 Quoted by E. A. Reitan (ed.), *George III: Tyrant or Constitutional Monarch?* (Boston, 1964), xii, xxi, 35.
2 Bonamy Dobrée (ed.), *The Letters of King George III* (New York, 1968), 95.
3 Romney Sedgewick (ed.), *Letters From George III to Lord Bute, 1756–66* (London, 1939), lx.
4 *Ibid.*, lx.
5 Stanley Ayling, *George the Third* (New York, 1972), 16.
6 John Brooke, *King George III* (New York, 1972), 25. This is the standard biography.
7 *Ibid.*, 28.
8 Sedgewick, *op. cit.*, 2–3.
9 *Ibid.*, 1.
10 Dobrée, *op. cit.*, 15.
11 Sedgewick, *op. cit.*, 47.
12 Dobrée, *op. cit.*, 247.
13 *Ibid.*, 19.
14 Sedgewick, *op. cit.*, lxvi.
15 *Ibid.*, 19.
16 Dobrée, *op. cit.*, 10.
17 *Ibid.*, 5.
18 *Ibid.*, 7.
19 Brooke, *op. cit.*, 61.
20 Dobrée, *op. cit.*, 105.
21 *Ibid.*, 35.
22 John Clarke, *The Life and Times of George III*, (London, 1971), 81.
23 Ida MacAlpine and Richard Hunter, *George III and the Mad-Business* (London, 1969), 14.
24 Nesta Pain, *George III at Home* (London, 1975), 24.
25 Brooke, *op. cit.*, 387.
26 *Ibid.*, ix.

VIII   Victoria

1 Viscount Esher, *The Girlhood of Queen Victoria, A Selection from Her*

Majesty's Diaries Between the Years 1832 and 1840 (London, 1912), I, 195–6. Henceforth cited as *Journal*.

2 Cecil Woodham-Smith, *Queen Victoria: From her Birth to the Death of the Prince Consort* (New York, 1972), 140.

3 *Journal*, I, 196–8.

4 Woodham-Smith, *op. cit.*, 33.

5 *Journal*, I, 136.

6 *Ibid.*, 166.

7 *Ibid.*, 193.

8 Woodham-Smith, *op. cit.*, 144.

9 Alison Plowden, *The Young Victoria* (London, 1981), 163.

10 Elizabeth Longford, *Queen Victoria: Born to Succeed* (New York, 1964), 70.

11 Woodham-Smith, *op. cit.*, 69.

12 Dulcie Ashdown, *Royal Children* (London, 1979), 150ff.

13 Longford, *op. cit.*, 59.

14 Woodham-Smith, *op. cit.*, 95.

15 *Ibid.*, 96.

16 Morris Marples, *Princes in the Making: A Study of Royal Education* (London, 1965), 156–78.

17 Woodham-Smith, *op. cit.*, 94.

18 Dorothy Marshall, *The Life and Times of Victoria* (New York, 1974), 18.

19 Woodham-Smith, *op. cit.*, 85.

20 *Journal*, I, 190.

21 Plowden, *op. cit.*, 171.

22 Longford, *op. cit.*, 323.

23 *Ibid.*, 452.

24 Woodham-Smith, *op. cit.*, 148.

25 Longford, *op. cit.*, 290.

26 Marples, *op. cit.*, 153.

27 Woodham-Smith, *op. cit.*, 330.

28 *Ibid.*, 396.

29 Marshall, *op. cit.*, 202.

30 *Ibid.*, 163.

IX   Edward VIII

1 J. Bryan and Charles J.V. Murphy, *The Windsor Story* (New York, 1979), 314.

2 Frances Donaldson, *Edward VIII* (London, 1976), ix.

3 Duke of Windsor, *A King's Story* (New York, 1951), 19–20.

4 *Ibid.*, 59.

5 Bryan and Murphy, *op. cit.*, 58.

6 Christopher Hibbert, *Edward: The Uncrowned King* (New York, 1972), 6.

7 Windsor, *op. cit.*, 81–3.

8 Stephen Birmingham, *Duchess: The Story of Wallis Warfield Windsor* (Boston, 1981), 73.
9 Donaldson, *op. cit.*, 42.
10 *Ibid.*, 47.
11 Windsor, *op. cit.*, 102.
12 *Ibid.*, 111–12.
13 Donaldson, *op. cit.*, 51.
14 L.W. Rosensweig, The Abdication of Edward VIII: a psychohistorical explanation', *Journal of British Studies*, 14 (1975), 102–19.
15 Harold Nicolson, *King George the Fifth* (London, 1952), 53.
16 Hibbert, *op. cit.*, 29.
17 Windsor, *op. cit.*, 28.
18 Mercifully the cancer prompted a sudden and massive heart attack whilst George VI was asleep.
19 Duke of Windsor, *A Family Album* (London, 1960), 39, 101. Published in the USA as *Windsor Revisited*.
20 Windsor, *A King's Story*, 24.
21 Denis Judd, *The Life and Times of George V* (London, 1973), 165.
22 Donaldson, *op. cit.*, 174.
23 Lord Beaverbrook, *The Abdication of Edward VIII* (New York, 1966), 13.
24 Windsor, *A King's Story*, 276.
25 Donaldson, *op. cit.*, 401.
26 *Ibid.*, 201.
27 Bryan and Murphy, *op. cit.*, 392.
28 Alistair Cooke, *Six Men* (New York, 1977), 72–82.
29 Donaldson, *op. cit.*, 201.
30 Brian Inglis, *Abdication* (New York, 1966), 25.
31 Windsor, *A King's Story*, 28.
32 Bryan and Murphy, *op. cit.*, 367.
33 Windsor, *A King's Story*, 257.
34 Inglis, *op. cit.*, 46.
35 Windsor, *A King's Story*, 359.
36 Bryan and Murphy, *op. cit.*, 69, 99. My thanks to Mr Bryan and Mr Murphy for confirming Mrs Dudley Ward's recollections in personal correspondence.
37 *Ibid.*, 511.
38 *Ibid.*, 583.

X   Ich Dien

1 Sir John Wheeler-Bennett, *King George VI: His Life and Reign* (New York, 1958), 293–4.
2 Robert Lacey, *Elizabeth II and the House of Windsor* (New York, 1977), 161.
3 Elizabeth Longford, *The Queen: The Life of Elizabeth II* (New York, 1983), 30.

4 Wheeler-Bennett, *op. cit.*, 754–5.
5 Marion Crawford, *The Little Princesses* (New York, 1958), 17.
6 *Ibid.*, 77.
7 Anthony Holden, *Prince Charles: A Biography* (New York, 1977), 98.
8 Longford, *op. cit.*, 69–71.
9 Crawford, *op. cit.*, 205.
10 *Ibid.*, 145.
11 *Ibid.*, 216.
12 *Ibid.*, 219.
13 Lacey, *op. cit.*, 149.
14 Christopher Hibbert, *The Court of St. James's: The Monarch at Work from Victoria to Elizabeth II* (New York, 1980), 220.
15 Wheeler-Bennett, *op. cit.*, 749.
16 *Ibid.*, 754–5.
17 Basil Boothroyd, *Prince Philip: An Informal Biography* (New York, 1971), 32.
18 Crawford, *op. cit.*, 311.
19 Holden, *op. cit.*, 117–26.
20 Longford, *op. cit.*, 228.
21 Dermot Morrah, *To Be a King* (London, 1968), 67.
22 Holden, *op. cit.*, 146–51.
23 Denis Judd, *Prince Philip: A Biography* (New York, 1981), 73.
24 *Ibid.*, 14.
25 Longford, *op. cit.*, 237.
26 Anthony Sampson, *The Changing Anatomy of Britain* (New York, 1982), 12.
27 Philip Ziegler, *Crown and People* (New York, 1978), 135–7.
28 *Ibid.*, 91.
29 J. Thompson and Arthur Mejia, *The Modern British Monarchy* (New York, 1971), 97.
30 Lacey, *op. cit.*, 281.
31 Holden, *op. cit.*, 218.

INDEX